ALWAYS Astonished

Selected Prose

by Fernando Pessoa

Edited, translated, and introduced by
Edwin Honig

City Lights Books
San Francisco

Front cover painting by Costa Pinheiro (detail)
Cover design by DiJiT
Book design by Patricia Fujii

Library of Congress Cataloging-in-Publication Data

Pessoa, Fernando, 1888-1935
    [Selections. English. 1988]
    Always astonished : selected prose / by Fernando Pessoa :
translated by Edwin Honig.
      p. cm.
    Translated from Portuguese.
    ISBN 0-87286-228-3 : $12.95
    1. Pessoa, Fernando, 1888-1935—Translations, English.
    I. Title.
PQ9261.P417A26 1988   88-16863
869.4'41—dc19   CIP

CITY LIGHTS BOOKS are edited by Lawrence Ferlinghetti and
Nancy J. Peters and published at the City Lights Bookstore,
261 Columbus Avenue, San Francisco, CA 94133.

 # Contents

(★Indicates original is written in English)

NOTE

The word order is sometimes changed in order to make the sense clearer, especially in sections originally written by Pessoa in English.

With the same purpose of clarifying meaning, words are occasionally added, and in such instances are set in brackets in the text.

Finally, in those instances where Pessoa's and his printer's punctuation appear eccentric and would cause confusion, the copy has silently been amended.

E.H.

Introduction

Some Words in the Entryway

I.

After looking for him in the poems, we search for him in the prose. The pursuit of the other in Pessoa's work is never-ending. The other contains the various fragments of an *I* that the poet tries to mask and reveal at the same time. Masking to unmask, dressing to undress—tricks actors learn in shifting with the action of the play from one phase of identity to another. In transforming these fragments of identity lies the whole meaning of the action—a message formulated in Pessoa's maxim, "To pretend is to know oneself."

By following his pursuit of himself, one observes the dramatic shifts experienced in his heteronymic role changes.* Again, it is like watching an actor's appearance, disappearance and reappearance—moving, say, between a wife's husband and lover and perhaps also between her and her husband earlier in their lives. The uncommonness of Pessoa's daring (starting as a schoolboy writing in English under the pseudonyms Alexander Search and Charles Robert Anon) is that he persisted all his life in being many others. It is as if, on the one hand, he were constantly giving birth to himself, and then alternatively allowing himself to be superseded out of existence—so as to become nothing. His best-known poem, "Tabacaria" ("Tobacco Shop"), begins:

---

*See II, 1, "The Genesis of My Heteronyms," following, for Pessoa's explanation of these categories.

I'm nothing,
I'll always be nothing.
I can't even wish to be something.
Aside from that, I've got all the world's
dreams inside me.

Or, as the exclusively prose-writing semiheteronym Bernardo Soares puts it, "In each of us there is a differingness and a manyness and a profusion of ourselves."

Pessoa's fictive reselvings are like the commonplaces of family succession. Having children is a way of remaking oneself. Parents seek as many versions of themselves as they can give issue to, hoping for clones so nearly identical that they become more like one than oneself. The wish is similarly to conjoin remnants of some illusory self with a new undiluted self against the disintegrations of time.

Part of his reselving process surely owes something to the suicide of a best friend, Mário de Sá-Carneiro, the poet who early on had instigated Pessoa's experiments with heteronymic identifications. Did the friend's suicide ultimately become a substitute sacrifice that kept Pessoa, who was undergoing a severe personality crisis, from going mad or killing himself?

Fernando Pessoa the lifelong bachelor had his family in the heteronyms. Pessoa the friend could experience the suicide of Sá-Carneiro through the unselving of his central persona, Caeiro, whose name is a condensation of Carneiro. In the act of killing off Caerio in 1919, he may have been following a desire to eternalize in his own lifetime a form of himself already being canonized and worshipped by the other heteronyms, Álvaro de Campos and Ricardo Reis.

The stratagem behind such metamorphoses has been tried but scarcely probed by modern poets casting off the subjective self: to cope with estranged fragments of poetic identity by making specific dramatic characters out of them, occasionally lifted from one's personal life. The essay on Shakespeare annotates his own case: a "hystero-neurasthenic" (Pessoa calls him) whose lyric gift creates variously fleshed dramatic personae who help to reorient his

ii

dislocated personality and give his art a raison d'être it could not otherwise have. The practice also serves to mute momentarily the disquieting problem of how to continue in a world inimical to poetic survival: Be not one poet but four or even nineteen!

When he wrote, "I am a nomadic wanderer through my consciousness," he was stating the condition of the post-Romantic who, finding no model in the past, was left to rummage through his consciousness for whatever guidance the search might generate. The sentence further implies that the alien "I" does not belong to "my consciousness," and hence is detached and something different from the central *I*. In pursuit of the other, the wanderer keeps translating the inscrutable messages of consciousness by impersonating, as translators do, the absent author himself, possibly to achieve some affective identification with a fictive self—perhaps a hypothetical former self, perhaps a self-to-be.

The heteronyms allow for travels in space, even if the space is the inside of the head, as the pretender travels in time: forward to self-perpetuation, backward to self-immolation. And the travels in space, through the intricate arena of the psyche, provide a way of being in two or ten places at once.

Sometimes in his wanderings the poet plays, or thinks he is being played, with intrusive moments of time that convey him out of the everyday world. Such moments may take the form of a dreadful epiphany of being "victoriously tried" by the Demon of Reality, as "the great men in life are" (see "Suddenly"). And this may be as close as Pessoa gets to experiencing the presence of outer guides.

The poet's actual guide, if not "my consciousness" itself, may involve the cultivating of one's sensations of the multiplex world, imminently intriguing to all the senses but ultimately without meaning to any. To overcome dread of the meaningless and the pain of enduring the loss of self, the poet is enjoined to "increase absurdly the suffering that will be felt." He must will to suffer consciously both pleasure and pain, "to give anxieties and sufferings, by an exacerbated application of one's attention, an intensity so great that it brings on, by its own excess, the pleasure of excess" ("Sentimental Education").

In this way he finds out how to ward off, by anticipating, what he fears. To anticipate suffering by feeling it beforehand gives him some chance of tricking or outwitting it—hence the pleasure of "excess." Pessoa's analysis of a suffering that promises the joy of experiencing and outwitting pain links him to the masochism of a Kafka. In a similar mood, Kafka's "In the Penal Colony" portrays a technician's detached view of inflicting pain and then undergoing it himself. The penal officer and his victim, the prisoner, are subject to the operations of the punishing machine, a grotesque contraption that with claws and needles writes the prisoner's sentence on his bare skin. When the machine breaks down, the prisoner is removed, and the officer puts himself under the disintegration mechanism to be crushed and macerated.

This confluence between the will to suffer excessively and a passionate belief in the punishing machine suggests that at some point artistic detachment and dismemberment partake of the same self-vacating operation. One thinks of the castrato emasculated as a boy to enable him to preserve and strengthen his soprano voice to produce pure sounds later. And one recalls the boy poet Arthur Rimbaud, who wanted to banish the restricting demands of the ego by systematically deranging his senses and getting rid of his central *I.* " 'Je' est un autre" (" 'I' is someone else") not only dissolves the poet's subjective self and prepares the way for dramatizing multiple personae but also sets up an ineluctable identification with the techniques and materials of one's art. "So much worse for the wood," Rimbaud remarks, "if it should find itself a violin"; and again, "If brass wakes up as a trumpet, that's not its fault."

According to the Orpheus myth, the dismembered body of the poet floats down the river into the sea, each fragment singing. Giordano Bruno wrote that Actaeon, punished by Diana's hounds for seeing her naked, enjoyed in each piece his being torn apart. The voice, the instrument, is everything, while the singer, the various parts of him, dissolves in song.

II

During his lifetime (1888–1935), Pessoa published mostly cultural and literary journalism. Starting signally in 1912 with three urgent essays on aspects of modern Portuguese life and letters, he went on to write articles for the newspapers and literary journals of Lisbon and Oporto. Some were signed by his heteronyms, Álvaro de Campos and Ricardo Reis, who occasionally defended their differences over aesthetic questions, even over the work of his prized major heteronym, Alberto Caeiro. Caeiro himself was exempted from writing in prose.

Since all his schooling had been in English, Pessoa wrote poetry in English exclusively during his early years (1901–09). Also begun early were his critical prose notes and short essays on classical and Renaissance philosophy (*Textos Filosóficos*) written in English and in Portuguese. His note-taking, started during his school days in Durban, continued throughout his life.

After deciding in 1909 to become a Portuguese writer, he joined a group of like-minded Lisbon intellectuals who started the magazine *A Águia* (1910–30). Thereafter, he wrote poems and discursive pieces in Portuguese but continued writing poetry in English until a few days before his death. With Mário de Sá-Carneiro, he was cofounder of the Orpheu group (1915) and its short-lived magazine of the same name, pledged to renew language, ideas, and beauty; then he was associated with its brief successor, *Portugal Futurista*.

His principal interest was to build a modernist position paralleling those being sounded out in France and Italy, and to generate a taste for his ideas, some of which were already being adopted internally in the works of his heteronyms. For a year or so he promoted *Paulismo*, a version of English and French decadent poetry, and then discarded it for *Interseccionismo*, a poetry based on a type of visual impressionism and ironic collapse, suggestive of the early work of Ezra Pound and that of John Gould Fletcher, writers he may not yet have heard of. But the type of literary and philosophical futurism he came to champion was *Sensacionismo*. Its principal exponents were Alberto Caeiro, the unschooled shepherd poet of total sense-feeling (*O Guardador de Rebanhos* [*The Keeper of Sheep*]) and Álvaro de Campos, the manic-depressive ship's engineer-poet of technology ("Ode Triumfal" ["Triumphal Ode"]), and of dissociated sensibility ("Tabacaria" ["Tobacco Shop"]).

The decade between 1910 and 1920 was Pessoa's most productive period. It coincided with a new surge of imaginative energy released by the formation of the Portuguese Republic in 1919 and by the eruptive influences of the First World War. In the twenties Pessoa's work began to be known by groups of the Lisbon literati. A younger generation of writers soon emerged and established a center through the magazine *Presença*, which promoted his work. His long and only complete story, "The Anarchist Banker," was published in 1922 in the magazine *Contemporânea*, and fragments of his journals were printed under the semiheteronym Bernardo Soares. Not until 1982, however, was all the Soares material assembled in a two-volume edition entitled *Livro de Desassosego* (*Book of Disquietude*).

Among his arch supporters were Armando Córtes-Rodrigues, the editor and literary critic, whose sympathies elicited Pessoa's revealing letters, including several crucial ones on the heteronyms; and João Gaspar Simões, the young novelist and critic whom Pessoa had befriended and instructed how to arrange his manuscripts, which Gaspar Simões then proceeded to prepare for publication on the poet's death. Of special importance subsequently was Gaspar Simões's pioneer study of Pessoa's life and work, *Vida e Obra de Fernando Pessoa* (1951).

Most of Pessoa's writings were left intact for future editors and scholars to parse and discuss. This material was deposited in his sister's Lisbon apartment, and there the archive remained, together with his library and papers, until recently, when it was transferred to the National Library. Today, on the centennial of his birth and with the major portion of the writings published, Pessoa has emerged as a full-fledged leading modernist the world over.

III

Like Kafka, Pessoa was at war with the body but mostly with the mind. Because his mind was his primary instrument in the war against himself, he kept sharpening it so that it could never cease to tell him how incapable he'd become of living in "the real world." The admission allowed him to believe the worst about himself and thus to become his own most powerful antagonist.

Pessoa comments on his horror of beginning anything, and then adds that he had the weakness of being unable to finish anything. Kafka says the same thing. The universe was an overwhelming enemy. Being orderly men with fearfully rational natures, how could they compete with all the world's daily disorganized energies and crushing super-reality long enough to create a completely functioning reality of their own, in art or in life? With their deeply-rooted self-enmity, they saw the world, their chief rival, as constantly threatening to explode into fragments.

When asked in 1968 if he'd read Kafka, Jorge Luis Borges said no. When asked if he'd read Pessoa, he replied, "Who is he?" Both were father or elder-brother figures, but Borges was not ready to learn from them or to succumb to their grossly masochistic survival tactics.

Borges, living in the dark of his growing blindness, might have learned from Kafka and Pessoa how to go forward and make of the fragments short fables that are complete entities, most inviting to puzzle-solvers. Borges's mirror of art startles readers into recognizing themselves as peers without having to succumb and grovel in a fatal Kafkan masochism or grim Pessoan disesteem. Borges offers a way out through an all-mastering mind; Kafka and Pessoa offer the mind as tasting and testing itself on a spit slowly roasting over a self-fueling fire.

IV

PESSOA'S LAST MASQUERADE

"Be admitted to the heart of your own
    self
dismissal," he proposed, choking on the effort
    to waken
the hidden one, the only shifter he kept
    subtracting,
more vehement, more drastic and diminished
    each day
than he'd admit. (Admit? To whom? His self-
    lessness?
The real self was his tool for scrutiny.)
    Lashed,
it cried, "Admit, admit!" but this he could
    not bear.

The shifter, now colliding with him, spat out:
    "Who are
you if not myself?" "Yourself—" he crowed,
    "therefore
a friend?" "Be nothing," it snapped at him
    again.
"Be yourself in silence but something less than
    a friend.
Be anything not your own, no selfless self-
    prolonger.
Practice a face for life's sake but be some-
    one else!"

A day to reckon with—he'd roused the last one
    just
to give it life and with this start something
    new:

viii

the opening to let them ... let out all
    the self
shifters fed daily on his remorseless words.
    Happening
so swiftly, so it passed, the last one
    to drift
way down through some pinpoint hole
    growing
in the remembered dark until he felt them all
    sucked in.

Then, with nothing to elude, nothing to feed
    in him,
the absence began—an absence, he saw, of all-
    become-him:
the one who might be, the one who was, the someone
    unborn
or long dead and never to come at him
    again.
Enemy friend admitted it, waking only
    for that,
with no words to forgive, as if even
    so little
were too much to give his briefly final
    being.

—Edwin Honig

Fernando Pessoa — Heterónimo

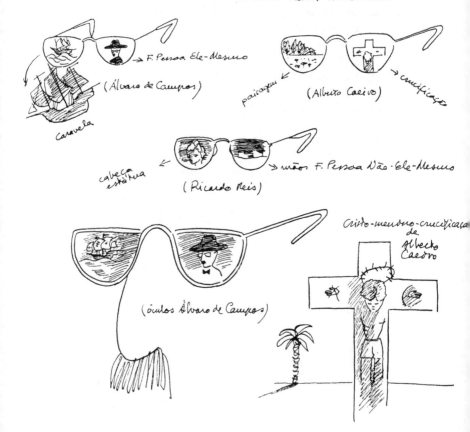

→ F. Pessoa Ele-Mesmo

(Álvaro de Campos)

Caravela

paisagem ←

(Alberto Caeiro)

→ crucificação

cabeça ←
estátua

(Ricardo Reis)

→ mãos F. Pessoa Não-Ele-Mesmo

(óculos Álvaro de Campos)

Cristo-menino-crucificação
de
Alberto
Caeiro

✖ Autobiographical Notes

1. [The earliest literary food]

The earliest literary food of my childhood was in the numerous novels of mystery and of horrible adventure. Those books, which are called boy's books and deal with exciting experiences, I cared little for. With a healthy and natural life I was out of sympathy. My craving was not for the probable, but for the incredible, not even for the impossible by degree, but for the impossible by nature.

My childhood was quiet (. . .), my education was good. But since I have [had] consciousness of myself, I have perceived in myself an inborn tendency to mystification, to artistic lying. Add to this a great love of the spiritual, of the mysterious, of the obscure, which, after all, was but a form and a variation of that other characteristic of mine, and my personality is, to intuition, complete.

1906

I was a poet animated by philosophy, not a philosopher with poetic faculties. I loved to admire the beauty of things, to trace in the imperceptible through the minute the poetic soul of the universe.

Poetry is in everything—in land and in sea, in lake and in riverside. It is in the city too—deny it not—it is evident to me here as I sit: there is poetry in this table, in this paper, in this inkstand; there is poetry in the rattling of cars on the streets, in each minute, common, ridiculous motion of a workman, who [on] the other side of the street is painting the sign-board of a butcher's shop.

1

Mine inner sense predominates in such a way over my five senses that I see things in this life—I do believe it—in a way different from other men. There is for me—there was—a wealth of meaning in a thing so ridiculous as a door key, a nail on the wall, a cat's whiskers. There is to me a fullness of spiritual suggestion in a fowl with its chickens strutting across the road. There is to me a meaning deeper than human fears in the smell of sandalwood, in the old tins on a dirt heap, in a match box lying in the gutter, in two dirty papers which, on a windy day, will roll and chase each other down the street. For poetry is astonishment, admiration, as of a being fallen from the skies taking full consciousness of his fall, astonished about things. As of one who knew things in their souls, striving to remember this knowledge, remembering that it was not thus he knew them, not under these forms and these conditions, but remembering nothing more.

1910

2. [It is necessary now]

It is necessary now that I should tell what manner of man I am. My name, it matters not, nor any other outward detail particular to me. Of my character aught must be said.

The whole constitution of my spirit is one of hesitancy and of doubt. Nothing is or can be positive to me; all things oscillate round me, and I with them, an uncertainty unto myself. All for me is incoherence and change. All is mystery and all is meaning. All things are "unknown" symbolic of the Unknown. Consequently horror, mystery, over-intelligent fear.

By my own natural tendencies, by the surroundings of my earliest life, by the influence of studies undertaken under the impulse of them (these very tendencies)—by all this I am of the internal species of character, self-centered, mute, not self-sufficing but self-lost. All my life has been one of passiveness and of dream. All my character consists in the hatred, in the horror of, in the incapacity pervading all that is me, physically and mentally, for decisive acts, for definite thoughts. I had never a resolution born of a self-command, never an external betraying of a conscious will. My writings were none of them finished; new thoughts intruded ever, extraordinary, inexcludable associations of ideas bearing infinity for term. I cannot prevent my thought's hatred of finish; about a single thing ten thousand thoughts, and ten thousand interassociations of these ten thousand thoughts arise, and I have no will to eliminate or to arrest these, nor to gather them into one central thought, where their unimportant but associated details may be lost. They pass in me; they are not my thoughts but thoughts that pass through me. I do not ponder, I dream; I am not inspired, I rave. I can paint, but I have never painted; I can compose music, but I have never composed. Strange conceptions in three arts, lovely strokes of imagining caress my brain; but I let them slumber there till they die, for I have not power to give them their body, to make them things of the world outside.

My character of mind is such that I hate the beginnings and the ends of things, for they are definite points. The idea of a solution being found for problems the highest, the noblest, of science, of philosophy, afflicts me; that aught might be determined of God or of the world horrorizes me. That things of most moment should be accomplished, that men should one day all be happy, that a solution might be found to the ills of society—[the ideas] even in its conception, maddens me. Yet I am not evil nor cruel; I am mad, and that, as it is [is] difficult to conceive.

Though I have been a reader voracious and ardent, yet I remember no book that I have read, so far were my reading states of my own mind, dreams of my own, nay, provocations of dreams. My very memory of events, of external things is vague, more than incoherent. I shudder to think how little I have in mind of what my past life has been. I, the man who holds that today is a dream, am less than a thing of today.

I have outgrown the habit of reading. I no longer read anything except occasional newspapers, light literature, and casual books technical to any matter I may be studying, and in which simple reasoning may be insufficient.

The definite type of literature I have almost dropped. I could read it for learning or for pleasure. But I have nothing to learn, and the pleasure to be drawn from books is of a type that can with profit be substituted by that which the contact with nature and the observation of life can directly give me.

I am now in full possession of the fundamental laws of literary art. Shakespeare can no longer teach me to be subtle, nor Milton to be complete. My intellect has attained a pliancy and a reach that enable me to assume any emotion I desire and to enter at will into any state of mind. For that which it is ever an effort and an anguish to strive for—completeness—no book at all can be an aid.

This does not mean that I have shaken off the tyranny of the literary art. I have but assumed it only under submission to myself.

There was a time when I read only for the use of reading. I now have understood that there are very few useful books, even in such technical matters as I can be interested in.

Sociology is wholesale . . .; who can stand this scholasticism in the byzantium of today?

All my books are books of reference. I read Shakespeare only in relation to the "Shakespeare Problem"; the rest I know already.

I have found out that reading is a slavish sort of dreaming. If I must dream, why not my own dreams?

1910

3. A Note on the Sexual Problem Preface (to be used for "Shakespeare"?)

I find no difficulty in defining myself: I am by temperament feminine with a masculine intelligence. My sensibility and the actions proceeding from it—and it is in this that a temperament and its expression consist—are feminine. My faculties of relationship—the intelligence and the will, which is the intelligence of impulse—are masculine.

As for sensibility, when I say that I always wanted to be loved and never to love, I've said it all. I always regretted being obliged by a common reciprocity—a loyalty of spirit—to respond.

Passivity pleased me. I was only content with activity just enough to stimulate me, not to let myself be forgotten—the activity of loving by one who loved me.

I have no illusions about the nature of the phenomenon. It is a repressed sexual inversion. It stops in the mind. Yet always, in moments of meditating about myself, I have been uneasy. I have never been sure, nor am I yet, that this temperamental disposition could not one day go down into my body. I am not saying that I would then practice the sexuality that corresponds to the impulse, but the desire to do so would be enough to humiliate me. Many of us of this type occur throughout history, especially through the history of art. Shakespeare and Rousseau are among the most famous examples or exemplars. An obsession with their cases being deeply rooted in me, my dread is that such mental inversion will take hold of the body—as with Shakespeare, completely, in the form of pederasty, or as with Rousseau, partially, in a vague form of masochism.

1915

✖ On the Heteronyms

1. The Genesis of My Heteronyms

. . . Into Caeiro I put all my power of dramatic depersonalization, into Ricardo Reis all my intellectual discipline, fashioned in the music appropriate to him, into Álvaro de Campos, all the emotion that I allow neither in myself nor in my living. To think, my dear Casais Monteiro, that all these must be, in terms of publication, overtakers of Fernando Pessoa, impure and simple!

. . . I now go on to answer your question about the genesis of my heteronyms. I am going to see if I can answer you fully.

I begin with the psychiatric part. The origin of my heteronyms is basically an aspect of hysteria that exists within me. I don't know whether I am simply a hysteric or if I am more properly a neurasthenic hysteric. I tend toward the second hypothesis, because there are in me evidences of lassitude that hysteria, properly speaking, doesn't encompass in the list of its symptoms. Be that as it may, the mental origin of my heteronyms lies in a persistent and organic tendency of mine to depersonalization and simulation. These phenomena—fortunately for me and others—intellectualize themselves. I mean, they don't show up in my practical life, on the surface and in contact with others; they explode inside, and I live with them alone in me. If I were a woman (in women hysterical phenomena erupt in attacks and in similar ways), each poem of Álvaro de Campos (or, more hysterically hysterical, of mine) would cause a riot in the neighborhood. But I am a man—and for us men hysteria assumes mainly intellectual aspects; so it all ends up in silence and poetry . . . .

This explains, *tant bien que mal,* the organic origin of my heteronyms. Now I'll tell you the straight story of my heteronyms. I begin with those who are dead, and with some I no longer remember—those that remain lost in the remote, almost forgotten past of my infancy. . . .

Since childhood I had the tendency to create around me a fictitious world, surrounding myself with friends and acquaintances that never existed. (I don't know, of course, if they really didn't exist or if it was I who didn't exist. In such matters, as in everything, we should not be dogmatic.) Since knowing myself to be the one I call myself, I remember fixing mentally by countenance, movement, character, and history, various unreal figures that were for me as visible as those we perhaps abusively call real-life. This tendency, present in me since I recall being an "I," has always accompanied me, muffling a bit the sort of music it enchants me with but never ceasing its manner of enchanting me.

So I remember what appears to me to have been my first heteronym, or rather my first nonexistent acquaintance—a certain Chevalier de Pas, when I was six years of age, from whom I wrote letters to myself, and whose figure, not completely vague, still dominates that part of my affection confined to longing. I remember, less clearly, another figure whose name no longer comes to mind, except that he was also a stranger who was, I don't know how, a rival of Chevalier de Pas. . . . Things that happen to all children? Perhaps, perhaps not. But during such a period I experienced them, as I still do, because I remember them in such a way that it requires some effort to realize they weren't real.

Such a tendency to create around me another world, equal to this one but with other people, never left my imagination. It had various phases, including this one, which now occurs in my maturity. An urging of spirit came upon me, absolutely foreign, for one reason or another, of that which I am, or which I suppose that I am. I spoke to it, immediately, spontaneously, as if it were a certain friend of mine whose name I invented, whose history I adapted, and whose figure—face, build, clothes, and manner—I immediately saw inside of me. And so I contrived and procreated various friends and acquaintances who never existed but whom still today—nearly

thirty years later—I hear, feel, see. I repeat: I hear, feel, see. . . .
And get greetings from them. . . .

Sometime around 1912, unless I'm mistaken (which I couldn't be by very much), the idea came to me to write a few poems of pagan character. I sketched out some things in free verse (not in the style of Álvaro de Campos but in a sort of half-normal style) and then abandoned the attempt. But in that dim confusion I made out the hazy outline of the person who was writing. (Without my knowing it, Ricardo Reis had been born.)

A year and a half or two years later, I recall one day taking up a challenge of Sá-Carneiro's—to invent a rather complicated bucolic poet and present him, I don't remember how, as if he were a really living creature. I spent a few days working on him but got nowhere. The day I finally gave up—it was March 8, 1914—I went over to a high desk and, taking a piece of paper, began to write, standing up, as I always do when I can. And I wrote some thirty poems, one after another, in a kind of ecstasy, the nature of which I am unable to define. It was the triumphant day of my life, and never will I have another like it. I began with the title, *The Keeper of Sheep*. What followed was the appearance of someone in me whom I named, from then on, Alberto Caeiro. Forgive me the absurdity of the sentence: In me there appeared my master. That was my immediate reaction. So much so that scarcely were those thirty-odd poems written when I snatched more paper and wrote, again without stopping, the six poems constituting "Oblique Rain," by Fernando Pessoa. Straight away and completely. . . . It was the return of Fernando Pessoa/Alberto Caeiro to Fernando Pessoa himself. Or better, it was the reaction of Fernando Pessoa against his nonexistence as Alberto Caeiro.

Once Alberto Caeiro appeared, I tried—instinctively and subconsciously—to find disciples for him. Out of his false paganism I plucked the latent Ricardo Reis, whose name I discovered and adapted to him, because at that stage I already had seen him there. And suddenly, deriving in opposition to Ricardo Reis, there impetuously arose in me a new individual. At once, and on the typewriter,

9

there surged up, without interruption or correction, the "Triumphal Ode" of Álvaro de Campos—the ode of that title and the man of that name.

I then created a nonexistent coterie. I arranged it all in real patterns. I gauged influences, I knew the friendships, I heard inside me the discussions and divergences of opinion, and in all this it seems that it was I, creator of it all, who was least present. It appears that everything went on independently of me. And it still seems to go on that way. If some day I can publish the aesthetic discussions between Ricardo Reis and Álvaro de Campos, you'll see how different they are and how I myself have nothing to do with the matter.

When *Orpheu* was about to be published, it was necessary at the last moment to delete something in order to come up with the right number of pages. I then suggested to Sá-Carneiro that I put in an "old" poem about what Álvaro de Campos would have been like before he'd known Caeiro and come under his influence. And so I made up the "Opium Eater," in which I attempted to present all the latent tendencies of Álvaro de Campos, in keeping with what would be revealed later, but without having as yet any hint of contact with his master Caeiro. It was out of the poems I've written, or that I got myself to make up, through the double power of depersonalization, that I had to develop. But in the end I don't believe the poem turned out too badly, and it does show Álvaro in the bud. . . .

I think I've explained to you the origin of my heteronyms. If some point remains that requires further clarification (I am writing fast, and when I write fast I am not very lucid), I intend in good time to fill you in on it. And it's true that really complementing it all is the hysterical, because in writing certain passages of the "Notes in Memory of My Master Caeiro," by Álvaro de Campos, I've wept real tears. This will let you know whom you have to deal with, my dear Casais Monteiro!

Some further comments about all this. . . . I *saw* before me in the colorless but real space of a dream the faces and gestures of Alberto Caeiro, Ricardo Reis, and Álvaro de Campos. I made out their ages and their lives. Ricardo Reis was born in 1887 (not that I remember the day and the month, though I have them somewhere) in Oporto, is a doctor, and is now living in Brazil. Alberto Caeiro was born in 1889 and died in 1915; he was born in Lisbon but lived nearly all his life in the country. He had no profession or any sort of education. Álvaro de Campos was born in Tavira, on the fifteenth of October, 1890 (at 1:30 P.M., Ferreira Gomes tells me, and it's true, because it's confirmed by a horoscope I made of this hour). As you know, he's a naval engineer (in Glasgow) but now lives here in Lisbon, unemployed. Caeiro was of medium height and, though delicate (he died a consumptive), he didn't seem as delicate as he was. Ricardo Reis is a bit, though very slightly, shorter, more robust, but shrewd. Álvaro de Campos is tall (1.75 meters tall, two centimeters taller than I), slender and with a slight tendency to stoop. All are clean-shaven: Caeiro pale, without color, blue eyes; Reis a vague dull brown; Campos between fair and swarthy, a vaguely Jewish-Portuguese type, hair therefore smooth and normally parted on the side, monocled. Caeiro, as I said, had no education to speak of—only primary school; his father and mother died early and he stayed at home, where he lived on the income of some small properties. He lived with an old aunt on his mother's side. Ricardo Reis is, as I said, a doctor; he has been living in Brazil since 1919; he became an expatriate immediately, because he was a monarchist. He is a Latinist by virtue of school training and a semi-Hellenist by virtue of his own efforts. Álvaro de Campos had a high-school education; he later went to Scotland to study engineering, first mechanical, than naval. On some holiday he went to the Orient, from which the "Opium Eater" is derived. An uncle, a priest from Beira, taught him Latin.

How do I write under these three names? . . . Caeiro, by way of pure and unexpected inspiration, without knowing or deliberately thinking of what I'd write. Ricardo Reis, after some abstract deliberation that suddenly concretizes itself in an ode. Campos, when I feel a sudden impulse to write and don't know what. (My semiheteronym Bernardo Soares, who in many ways resembles Álvaro de Campos, seems always to be tired or sleepy, so that his powers of ratiocination and his inhibitions are slightly suspended; he writes prose in a constant daydream. He is a

semiheteronym because, not being a personality to me, he is not so much different from myself as he is a simple distortion of my personality. It is myself, less rational and less emotional. [It is] prose, except for what reason attenuates in mine, [. . .] equal to mine, and the Portuguese, completely the same. As far as that's concerned, Caeiro wrote Portuguese badly; Campos, reasonably but with lapses, as when he would say *eu propio* instead of *eu mesmo*, etcetera; Reis, better than I but with a puristic streak that I regard as exaggerated. It's difficult for me to write the prose of Reis—still unedited—or of Campos. Simulating in verse is easier, because it is more spontaneous.)   (From the letter to Adolfo Casais Monteiro,
dated January 13, 1935)

2. Presenting the Heteronyms
(Aspects: Preface to the Projected Edition of his Works)

The Complete Work, of which this is the first volume, is dramatic in substance, although varied in form—prose pieces here, poems or philosophies in the other books. And as for the frame of mind that produced it, I don't know if that's a talent or a sickness. But in any case, the fact certainly is that the author of these lines—I don't quite know if he is the author of these books—never had a single personality or ever thought or felt except dramatically, that is, through a fictitious person who could have these feelings more than he himself ever could.

There are authors who write plays and novels, and in such plays and novels assign feelings and ideas to the characters who inhabit the works; these same authors are annoyed that such feelings or ideas should be taken for their own. Here the substance is the same, although the form is different.

To each personality that the author of these books slowly evolved within himself he gave an expressive temperament and made of that personality an author with a book or books; in those ideas, emotions, and art, he, the real author (or perhaps apparent author, as we don't know what reality is), never played any part,

12

except insofar as he was, in the writing of them, the medium of the characters he himself created.

Neither in this work nor in those that will follow is anything to be seen of him who writes them. He neither agrees nor disagrees with what is written in them. He writes just as it was dictated to him, and, as if it were dictated by a friend—who therefore has some reason to ask that he write what is said—he thinks interesting (perhaps by virtue of the friendship) that which, dictated, he keeps writing.

The human author of these books does not recognize in himself any personality whatever. When by chance he feels a personality emerge in himself, he soon sees that it is a being different from his own, although similar—a mental offspring, perhaps, with inherited characteristics but by having the differences of someone else.

That this attribute of the writer may be a form of hysteria or of a so-called dissociation of personality, the author of these books neither opposes nor favors. Enslaved as he is to the multiplicity of himself, it would be of no use at all to him to support this or that theory concerning the written products of such multiplicity.

It is not surprising that such a process of producing art seems strange; the surprising thing is that he should make anything that is not strange.

Some theories that the author presently holds were inspired by one or another of these personalities who, for an instant, an hour, or even longer, were consubstantiated in his own personality, if such exists.

To affirm that these men—all different, all well defined, who pass bodilessly through his soul—do not exist, the author of these books cannot maintain, because he does not know what existing is, or which one, Hamlet or Shakespeare, is more real, or real in truth.

Meanwhile, the books in question are the following: first, this volume, *Book of Disquietude,* written by one who wished to call himself Vicente Guedes; then, *The Keeper of Sheep and Other Poems and Fragments,* by Alberto Caeiro (also, and in the same manner, grown scarce), born near Lisbon in 1889 and died where he was born in 1915. If I'm then told that it's absurd to speak of someone who never existed, I reply that neither do I have proof that Lisbon ever existed or that I who write exist, or that anything does, whatever it is.

This Alberto Caeiro had two disciples and one follower in philosophy. The two disciples, Ricardo Reis and Álvaro do Campos, took different paths: the first intensified and turned artistically orthodox the paganism discovered by Caeiro, and the second, basing himself on another part of the work of Caeiro, developed a quite different system rooted wholly in sensation. The follower in philosophy, Antônio Mora (the names are inevitable, being imposed from without, as the personalities are), has one or two books to write in which he will demonstrate completely the metaphysical and practical truth of paganism. A second philosopher of this pagan school, whose name, however, has not yet appeared before my vision or inner hearing, will defend paganism on entirely different grounds and with other arguments.

It is possible that other individuals of this same genre of authentic reality will emerge later. I don't know; but they will always be welcome to my inner life, where they live with me better than I manage to live with outer reality. Needless to say, I agree with some of their theories and disagree with other aspects. These matters are perfectly unimportant. If they write beautiful things, such things are beautiful independent of any sort of metaphysical considerations of their "real" authors. If in their philosophies they speak whatever kind of truths—if truths there be in a world that is one of having nothing—such truths are independent of the intention or of the "reality" of him who utters them.

Transforming myself in this manner—at least a madman with lofty dreams, at most not a single writer but a whole literature, when not adding to my own entertainment, which would quite suffice me—I perhaps add to the enhancement of the universe, because whoever at his death leaves behind one beautiful line of verse leaves the skies and the earth richer and the reason for there being stars and people more emotionally mysterious.

With such a paucity of literature as exists today, what can a man of genius do but transform himself—himself alone—into a literature? With such a paucity of coexistent people as exist nowadays, what can a man of sensibility do but invent his friends, or at least his companions of the spirit?

I thought at first of publishing these works anonymously, with regard to myself, and by example to establish a Portuguese neopaganism with various authors, all different, to collaborate and propagate it. But as the Portuguese intellectual milieu is all too sparse and quite without confidence to sustain the level, the mental effort needed to maintain it would prove futile.

In what I call my inner vision—only because I call the fixed "world" external—I have fully determined (clearly, recognizably, distinctly) the physiognomic lines, the traces of character, the life, the genealogy and, in some instances, the death dates of this cast of characters. Some were acquainted with one another; others, not. Not one of them knew me personally save Álvaro de Campos. But if on a trip to America tomorrow I should suddenly run into the physical presence of Ricardo Reis, who in my view is alive there, no sign of surprise would escape my soul to my body. It has all been vouchsafed, and even before that already vouchsafed. What is life?

1930

3. A Note on the Works

The series or collection of books begun with the publication of what follows is not a new procedure in literature but a new way of employing an already old procedure.

I want to be a creator of myth, which is the highest mystery that anyone can make out of humankind.

Putting together these works does not manifest any particular kind of metaphysical opinion. I mean that in writing these "aspects" of reality concretized in people who might have had them, I do not intend a philosophy that implies there is only reality in possessing such aspects of reality either illusory or nonexistent. I neither possess nor oppose such a philosophic belief. In my craft, which is literary, I am a professional, in the superior sense that the term possesses; that is, I am a scientific worker who does not allow strange opinions to enter into his literary specialization and take him over. And in not having one or another philosophical opinion associated with putting together such person-books, neither would I imply that I am a skeptic. The question exists on a plane where metaphysical speculation, because it does not legitimately enter, is exempt from having these or other characteristics. Just as physics (the physical has no metaphysics in its laboratory) does not admit the clinical in the diagnoses it makes, not because it is not able to but because . . . so *my* metaphysical problem does not exist, because it can't, nor does it have to exist inside the covers of these, my books by others.

1930

4. Alberto Caeiro, the Master
a. Introduction to Alberto Caeiro's Poems
by Ricardo Reis

To whom can Caeiro be compared? To very few poets. Not, be it at once said, to that Cesário Verde to whom he refers as if to a literary ancestor. . . . Cesário Verde had on Caeiro the kind of influence which may be called merely provocative of inspiration, without handing on any kind of inspiration. An example familiar to the reader is Chateaubriand's very real *influence* on Hugo, a man totally different, personally, literarily, and socially. . . .

The very few poets to whom Caeiro may be compared, either because he merely reminds, or might remind, us of them, or because he may be conceived of as having been influenced by them, whether we think [it] seriously or not, are Whitman, Francis Jammes and Teixeira de Pascoaes.

He resembles Whitman most. He resembles Francis Jammes on some secondary points. He reminds us strongly of Pascoaes because his attitude toward Nature is essentially a metaphysical, a naturalistic, and what may be called an absorbed attitude, as is that of Pascoaes, yet Caeiro is all that, inverting what Pascoaes is in the same way.

16

Caeiro, like Whitman, leaves us perplexed. We are thrown off our critical attitude by so extraordinary a phenomenon. We have never seen anything like it. Even after Whitman, Caeiro is strange and terribly, appallingly new. Even in our age, when we believe nothing can astonish us or shout novelty at us, Caeiro does astonish and does breathe absolute novelty. To be able to do this in an age like ours is the definite and final proof of his genius.

He is so novel that it is sometimes hard to conceive clearly [of] all his novelty. He is too new, and his excessive novelty troubles our vision of him, as all excessive things trouble vision, though it is quite a novelty for novelty itself to be the thing, to be excessive and vision-troubling. But that is the remarkable thing. Even novelty and the way of being new are novelties in Caeiro. He is different from all poets in another way than all great poets are different from other great poets. He has his individuality in another way of having it than all poets preceding him. Whitman is quite inferior in this respect. To explain Whitman, even on a basis [of] admitting him all conceivable originality, we need but think of him as an intense liver (lover?) of life, and his poems come out of that like flowers from a shrub. But the same method does not hold about Caeiro. Even if we think of him as a man who lives outside civilization (an impossible hypothesis, of course), as a man of an exceptionally clear vision of things, that does not logically produce in our minds a result resembling *The Keeper of Sheep*. The very tenderness for things as mere things which characterizes the type of man we have supposed (posited) does not characterize Caeiro. He sometimes speaks tenderly of things, but he asks our pardon for doing so, explaining that he only speaks so in consideration of our "stupidity of senses," to make us feel "the absolutely real existence" of things. Left to himself, he has no tenderness for things, he has hardly any tenderness even for his sensations. Here we touch his great originality, his almost inconceivable objectiveness (objectivity). He sees things with the eyes only, not with the mind. He does not let any thoughts arise when he looks at a flower. Far from seeing sermons in stones, he never even lets himself conceive [of] a stone as beginning a sermon. The only sermon a stone contains for him is that it exists. The only thing a stone tells him is that it has nothing at all to tell him. A state

17

of mind may be conceived resembling this. *But it cannot be conceived in a poet.* This way of looking at a stone may be described as the totally unpoetic way of looking at it. The stupendous fact about Caeiro is that out of this sentiment, or rather, absence of sentiment, he makes poetry. He feels positively what hitherto could not be conceived [of] except as a negative sentiment. Put it to yourselves: What do you think of a stone when you look at it without thinking about it? [It] comes to this: What do you think of a stone when you don't think about it at all? The question is quite absurd, of course. The strange point about it is that all Caeiro's poetry is based upon [a] sentiment that you find it impossible to represent to yourself as able to exist. Perhaps I have not been unsuccessful in pointing out the extraordinary nature of Caeiro's inspiration, the phenomenal novelty of his poetry, the astonishing unprecedentedness of his genius, of his whole attitude.

Alberto Caeiro is reported to have regretted the name . . . "sensationism," which a disciple of his—a rather queer disciple, it is true, Mr. Álvaro de Campos—gave to his attitude, and to the attitude he created. If Caeiro protested against the word as possibly seeming to indicate a "school," like Futurism, for instance, he was right, and for two reasons. For the very suggestion of schools and literary movements sounds bad when applied to so uncivilized and natural a kind of poetry. And besides, though he has at least two "disciples," the fact is that he has had on them an influence equal to that which some poet—Cesário Verde, perhaps—had on him: Neither resembles him at all; though, indeed, far more clearly than Cesário Verde's influence [on] him, his influence may be seen all over their work.

But the fact is—these considerations once put aside—that no name could describe his attitude better. His poetry is "sensationist." Its basis is the substitution of sensation for thought, not only as a basis of inspiration—which is comprehensible—but as a means of expression, if we may so speak. And, be it added, those two disciples of his, different as they are from him and from each other, are also indeed sensationists. For Dr. Ricardo Reis, with his neoclassicism, his actual and real belief in the existence of the pagan deities, is a pure sensationist, though a different kind of sensationist. His attitude toward nature is as aggressive to thought as Caeiro's; he reads no meanings into things. He sees them only, and if he seems to see them differently from Caeiro it is because, though seeing them as unintellectually and unpoetically as Caeiro, he sees them through a definite religious concept of the universe—paganism, pure paganism—and this necessarily alters his very direct way of feeling. But he is a pagan because paganism is *the* sensationist religion. Of course, a pure and integral sensationist like Caeiro has, logically enough, no religion at all, religion not being among the immediate data of pure and direct sensation. But Ricardo Reis has put the logic of his attitude as purely sensationist very clearly. According to him, we not only should bow down to the pure objectivity of things (hence his sensationism proper and his neoclassicism, for the classic poets were those who commented least, at least directly, upon things), but bow down to the equal objectivity, reality, naturalness of the necessities of our nature, of which the religious sentiment is one. Caeiro is the pure and absolute sensationist who bows down to sensations qua exterior and admits no more. Ricardo Reis is less absolute; he bows down also to the primitive elements of our own nature, our primitive feelings being as real and natural to him as flowers and trees. He is therefore religious. And, seeing that he is a sensationist, he is pagan in his religion, which is due not only to the nature of sensation once conceived of as admitting a religion of some kind, but also to the influence of those classical readings to which his sensationism had inclined him.

Álvaro de Campos, curiously enough, is, on the opposite point, entirely opposed to Ricardo Reis. Yet he is, not less than the latter, a disciple of Caeiro and a sensationist proper. He has accepted from Caeiro, not the essential and objective, but the deducible and subjective, part of his attitude. Sensation is all, Caeiro holds, and thought is a disease. By *sensation* Caeiro means the sensation of things as they are, without adding to it any elements from personal thought, convention, sentiment, or any other soul-place. For Campos, sensation is indeed all, but not necessarily sensation of things as they are, but of things as they are felt. So that he takes sensation subjectively and applies all his efforts, once so thinking, not to develop in himself the sensation of things as they are, but all sorts of sensations of things, even of the same thing. To feel is all: it is logical to conclude that the best is to feel all sorts of things in all sorts of ways, or, as Álvaro de Campos says himself, "to feel everything in every way." So he applies himself to feeling the town as much as he feels the country, the normal as he feels the abnormal, the bad as he feels the good, the morbid as the healthy. He never questions, he feels. He is the undisciplined child of sensation. Caeiro has one discipline: Things must be felt as they are. Ricardo Reis has another kind of discipline: Things must be felt, not only as they are, but also so as to fall in with a certain ideal of classic measure and rule. In Álvaro de Campos things must simply be felt.

But the common origin of these three widely different aspects of the same theory is patent and manifest.

Caeiro has no ethics except simplicity. Ricardo Reis has a pagan ethics, half epicurean and half stoic, but a very definite ethics, which gives his poetry an elevation that Caeiro himself, mastership apart, although the greater genius, cannot attain. Álvaro de Campos has no shadow of an ethics; he is non-moral, if not positively immoral, for, of course, according to his theory, it is natural that he should love the stronger better than the weak sensations, and the strong sensations are, at least, all selfish, and occasionally the sensations of cruelty and lust. Thus, Álvaro de Campos resembles Whitman most of the three. But he has nothing of Whitman's camaraderie: He is always apart from the crowd, and when feeling with them, it is very clearly and confessedly to please himself and [to] give himself brutal sensations. The idea that a child of eight is demoralized ("Ode 2" ad finem) ["Ode Triunfal"] is positively pleasant to him, for [that] idea . . . satisfies two very strong sensations—cruelty and lust. The most Caeiro says that may be called immoral is that he cares nothing for what men suffer, and that the existence of sick people is interesting because it is a fact. Ricardo Reis has nothing of this. He lives in himself, with his pagan faith and his sad epicureanism, but one of his attitudes is precisely not to hurt anyone. He cares absolutely nothing for others, not even

20

enough to be interested in their suffering or in their existence. He is moral because he is self-sufficient.

It may be said, comparing these three poets with the three orders of religious spirits, and comparing sensationism for the moment (perhaps improperly) with a religion, that Ricardo Reis is the normal religious spirit of that faith; Caeiro, the pure mystic; Álvaro de Campos, the ritualist in excess. For Caeiro loses sight of Nature in nature, loses sight of sensation in sensation, loses sight of things in things. And Campos loses sight of sensation in sensations.

1917

b. Alberto Caeiro: Translator's preface
by Ricardo Reis

At first sight it seems that something of Whitman is present in these poems. I have no information as to Caeiro's knowledge of foreign languages, or of English and of Whitman particularly; yet, on the face of it, and after a very cursory reading of the poems, I suspect the first to have been, at best, very slight; and the second and third, nil. However it may be, on close examination there is really no influence of Whitman here. There is at most an occasional coincidence, and the coincidence is merely of tone, and more apparent, therefore, than real. The essential difference is enormous.

The traits common to the two poets are the love of Nature and simplicity, and the astonishing acuity of sensation. But, whereas Whitman insistently reads transcendental meaning into Nature, nothing can be further from Caeiro's attitude than that; it is, as a matter of fact, the exact opposite to this attitude. And, whereas Whitman's sensations are immensely various and include both natural and artificial, and the metaphysical as well as the physical, Caeiro's persistently exclude even the more "natural artificial" things and are only metaphysical in that extremely peculiar negative manner which is one of the novelties of his attitude.

Again, Caeiro has a perfectly definite and coherent philosophy. It may not be as coherent in word and phrase as might be wished from a philosopher; but he is not a philosopher; [he is] a poet. It may not be coherent from the outset, but it grows more and more definite as we read on until, in the final poems of *The Keeper of Sheep,* it takes a definite and unmistakable shape. It is a quite perfectly defined absolute objectivism—the completest system of absolute objectivism which we have ever had, either from philosopher or from writer. There is philosophy in Whitman, but it is the philosophy of a poet and not of a thinker; and where there is philosophy it is not of an original cast, the sentiment alone being original. Not so in Caeiro, in whom both thought and feeling are altogether novel.

Finally, though both are "sensationists," Caeiro's sensationism is of a type different from Whitman's. The difference, though it seems subtle and difficult to explain, is nevertheless quite clear. It lies chiefly in this: Caeiro seizes on a single subject and sees it clearly; even when he seems to see it in a complex way, it will be found that [this] is but some means to see it all the more clearly. Whitman strives to see, not clearly, but deeply. Caeiro sees only the object, striving to separate it as much as possible from all other objects and from all sensations or ideas not, so to speak, part of the object itself. Whitman does the exact contrary: He strives to link up [the] object with all others, with many others, with the soul and the Universe and God.

Lastly, the very temperaments of the two poets differ. Even when he thinks, Whitman's thought is a mode of his feeling, or absolutely a mood, in the common decadent sense. Even when Caeiro feels, his feeling is a mode of his thought.

This description of their differences might be prolonged indefinitely. Whitman's violent democratic feeling could be contrasted with Caeiro's abhorrence for any sort of humanitarianism, Whitman's interest in all things human, with Caeiro's indifference to all that men feel, suffer, or enjoy.

After all, and all things considered, when we eliminate the superficial resemblance derived from [the] nonrhythmical character of the poetry of both men, and the abstract revolt against civilization, the resemblances between them are exhausted.

Besides, Whitman has really a sense of metrical rhythm; it is of a special kind, but it exists. Caeiro's rhythm is noticeably absent. He is so distinctly intellectual that the lines have no wave of feeling from which to derive their rhythmical movement.

What, after all, is Caeiro's value, his message to us, as the phrase goes? It is not difficult to determine. To a world plunged in various kinds of subjectivisms, he brings Absolute Objectivism, more absolute than the pagan objectivists ever had it. To a world over-civilized, he brings Absolute Nature back again. To a world merged in humanitarianisms, in workers' problems, in ethical societies, in social movements, he brings an absolute contempt for the fate and the life of man, which, if it be thought excessive, is at least natural to him and a magnificent corrective. Wordsworth had opposed natural man to artificial man; "natural man" is, for Caeiro, as artificial as anything else except Nature.

Our first impression of Caeiro is that everybody knows what he tells us, that there is therefore no need to say it. But it is the old story of Columbus' egg. If everybody knows this, why has no one said it? If not worth saying, but true, why has every poet said the contrary?

c. Notes on the Memory of My Master Caeiro
by Álvaro de Campos

I knew my master Caeiro under exceptional circumstances—as with all of life's circumstances, and especially those that, not being anything in themselves, have all to be seen as related in their consequences.

I left my Scottish course in naval engineering almost three quarters of the way through; I went off on a voyage to the Orient; on my way back, disembarking in Marseilles and feeling a great disinclination to continue, I proceeded by land to Lisbon. One day I was taken by a cousin of mine on an excursion to the Ribatejo; he knew a cousin of Caeiro's and had some business with him; I met the one who was to be my master in that cousin's house. There is not much to tell, because like all fecundations it's a small matter.

I still see with a clarity of mind that memory's tears do not blur, because the vision is not external. . . . I see it in front of me. I

23

see it perhaps eternally, as seen for the first time. First, the blue eyes of a child who is not afraid; then, the cheekbones already a bit prominent, complexion rather pale, with a strange Greek cast that was all calmness come from within, and not as an outer expression of facial features. The hair, rather thick, was blond, but away from the light it turned brown. He was of medium height, seeming taller, more stooped, not having high shoulders. His aspect was white, his smile such as it was, his voice the same, projected in the tone of one who cannot try to say anything but what he is saying—neither high nor low, clear, free of design, hesitation, or timidity. His blue glance was nothing if not fixed. If our observation found anything strange, he met it; his brow, without being high, was powerfully white. I repeat: It was this whiteness, seeming more intense than his pallid face, that gave him majesty. His hands rather slender, but not noticeably; his palm was large. The expression of his mouth, the last thing one noticed—as if for this man speaking was less than being—was like a smile one attributes in verse to beautiful inanimate things, a smile meant simply to please us—flowers, lush meadows, sunlit water—a smile of existence, not of speech.

Master mine, dear master, lost so soon! I see you again in the shadow that I am to myself, in the memory I conserve of I who am dead. . . .

It was during our first conversation. . . . How it came about I don't know, and he said: "That young fellow there, Ricardo Reis, who's a pleasure to meet—he is quite different from himself." And then he added, "Everything is different from us, and that's why everything exists."

The sentence, spoken like an axiom of the earth, overtook me like an earth tremor, like all first possessions, striking the rock bottom of my soul. But contrary to material seduction, its effect on me was suddenly to feel through all my senses a virginity I'd never experienced before.

Referring once to the direct apprehension of things characteristic of Caeiro's sensibility, I quoted with friendly perversity what Wordsworth designated as insensate in the expression

24

A primrose by the river's brim
A yellow primrose was to him,
And it was nothing more.

And I translated (omitting to translate primrose exactly, since I didn't know the names of flowers or plants), "A flower by the river's brim/ A yellow flower was for him,/ And it was nothing more."

My master Caeiro laughed. "That simple man saw well: a yellow flower is really nothing more than a yellow flower."

But suddenly he was thoughtful.

"There's a difference," he added, "depending on whether you consider the yellow flower to be one of various yellow flowers or just that yellow flower itself."

And then he said:

"What your English poet meant is that for such a man that yellow flower was an ordinary experience, or a well-known thing. But now that's not good. Everything we see should always be seen for the first time, because it is really the first time we see it. And so every yellow flower is a new yellow flower, even though it's called the same one as yesterday's. People now aren't the same; nor is the flower the same. The yellow itself can't now be the same. And it's a pity people don't have the exact same eyes to know that, because then we'd all be happy."

My master Caeiro was not a pagan; he was paganism. Ricardo Reis is a pagan, Antônio Mora is a pagan, I am a pagan; Fernando Pessoa himself would be a pagan, if he weren't such a tangled mess inside himself. But Ricardo Reis is a pagan by character, Antônio Mora by intelligence; I am a pagan by virtue of rebelliousness, that is, by temperament. With Caeiro there is no explanation for his paganism; it was a consubstantiation.

I'm going to define this the way one defines indefinable things—by cowardly example. One of the things that most clearly distinguishes us in comparison with the Greeks is the absence of the concept of infinity, the repugnance for infinity, among the Greeks.

Now my master Caeiro, in that regard, had such a concept. I'm going to relate, with what I believe is great precision, the surprising conversation in which he revealed it to me.

He was telling me, while referring to one of his poems in *The Keeper of Sheep,* that he didn't know who had once called him a "materialist poet." Although not finding the phrase justifiable, because my master Caeiro is not definable in any specific term, I said that the attribution wasn't at all absurd. And I explained to him, more or less well, what Greek materialism is. Caeiro heard me out with an attentive but pitying look and brusquely said to me:

"But it's just that that's so stupid. It's something to do with priests who have no religion, and it's therefore without any excuse whatever."

I was surprised and pointed out to him various similarities between materialism and his own doctrine, except for the poetry based on the latter. Caeiro protested.

"But what you call poetry is what everything is. It's not in poetry, it's in seeing. Materialists are blind people. You said they say that space is infinite. Where do they see that in space?"

And I, thrown off course: "But don't you think of space as infinite? Aren't you able to conceive of space as infinite?"

"I don't conceive of anything as infinite. How could I go about thinking anything infinite?"

"People," I said, "take space for granted. Beyond that space there's more space. Beyond that, more, and more again, and again. . . . It doesn't end."

"Why?" my master Caeiro replied.

I experienced a mental earthquake. "Suppose it ends," I cried, "what's there beyond?"

"If it ends, then nothing is beyond," he said.

This sort of argument, on the whole childlike and feminine and nevertheless unanswerable, numbed my mind a few moments.

"But is that what you think?" I finally let fall.

"Think what? That a thing has limits? Goodness! A thing without limits doesn't exist. To exist is to be something else, and therefore everything is limited. Why is it so hard to conceive that a

26

thing is a thing and is not always something else out there beyond it?"

At this point I had the physical sensation of speaking not with another man but with another universe. I made a last effort, taking a detour I obliged myself to feel was legitimate.

"Listen, Caeiro. . . . Think of numbers. Let's take any number—34, for example. Beyond that we have 35, 36, 37, 38, and so on, with no end in view. There's no large number without having a larger number following. . . ."

"But that's only numbers," my master Caeiro protested.

And then he added, looking at me in a formidable, childlike way, "What is the number 34 in reality?"

There are certain sentences, profound because they come from deep down, that define a man, or rather, by which a man defines himself without doing so. I won't forget that time Ricardo Reis once defined himself for me. He was speaking of lying, and he said, "I detest a lie because it is imprecise." All of Ricardo Reis—past, present, and future—is right there.

My master Caeiro, though I have spoken only of what he was, could be defined by any phrase of his, written or spoken—above all, after the period that begins halfway through *The Keeper of Sheep*. But among the many phrases he wrote or printed, among the many he spoke to me and I report or don't report, that which contains the greatest simplicity is the one he once spoke to me in Lisbon. He was talking of what I don't know, of things each of which I had to see with relation to itself. And I suddenly asked my master Caeiro, "Are you satisfied with yourself?" And he replied, "No, I am satisfied." It was like the voice of the earth that is everything and nothing.

I never saw my master Caeiro unhappy. I don't know if he was unhappy when he died or during the days previous. It would be possible to know that, but the truth is that I never dared ask those who were present anything about his death or how he died.

In any case, it was one of the sorrows of my life—the real sorrow among so many fictitious ones—that Caeiro should die without my being at his side. Such stupidity on my part is more human, and so be it.

I was in England; Ricardo Reis himself was not in Lisbon, he was on his way back to Brazil. Fernando Pessoa was there, but it was as though he was not. Fernando Pessoa feels things but doesn't react, not even inwardly.

Nothing consoles me for not having been in Lisbon that day, for not being that consolation which thinking of my master Caeiro spontaneously gives me. Nobody remains inconsolable having experienced the intimacy of the memory of Caeiro or his poems, and the very idea of nothingness—the most frightening of all ideas when thought of with feeling—has, in his work and in my dear master's memory, something of the luminosity and loftiness about it of the sun and the snowcapped mountaintops.

d. Preface to the *Fictions of the Interlude*

Astrologers attribute the effects in all things to the operation of four elements—fire, water, air, and earth. In this sense we'll be able to understand the operation of the influences. Some act on men like the earth, burying them and nullifying them, and those are the mandates of the world. Some act on men like the air, enveloping them and hiding them from one another, and these are the mandates of the world beyond. Some act on men like water, drenching and converting them into its own substance, and those are the ideologues and the philosophers that scatter among others the energies of their own soul. Some act on men like fire that burns out all the accidental in them and leaves them naked and real, individual and truthful, and those are the liberators. Caeiro is of that race. Caeiro had that force. What does it matter that Caeiro came out of me if Caeiro is like that?

So, operating on Reis, who still hadn't written a thing, he caused to be born an individual form and an aesthetic person. So, operating on me myself, he freed me from shadows and trash, gave my inspiration more inspiration and my soul more soul. After all that, so prodigiously accomplished, who will ask if Caeiro existed?

1916

e. A Conversation Between Álvaro de Campos and Ricardo Reis (excerpt)

Álvaro de Campos

Poetry is that form of prose in which rhythm is artificial.

But ask yourself: Why must one have artificial rhythm? The answer is: Because intense emotion does not fit the word. It must either fall into a scream or rise into a song. And as saying is speaking, and one cannot simultaneously scream and speak, one must sing speaking and put speech into music; and, as music is foreign to speech, music is put to speech, the words arranged so that they contain a music that is not in them, that must then be artificial in relation to them. And this is what poetry is: singing without music. That's why the great lyric poets, in the grand sense of the adjective "lyric," are not musical. How could they be lyric if they were musical?

Ricardo Reis

Campos says that poetry is prose in which the rhythm is artificial. He regards poetry as prose that involves music; hence the artifice. I, however, would say rather that poetry is music made with ideas and therefore with words. Imagine what your making music with ideas instead of with emotions would be like. With emotion you make only music. With emotion that tends toward ideas, that accumulates ideas in order to define themselves, you create song. With ideas alone, which contain only that part of emotion that is necessarily in all ideas, you make poetry. And therefore song is the primitive form of poetry, because it is the way for it to go—or, it is not the original form of poetry but the way toward it.

The cooler the poetry, the truer it is. Emotion should not enter into poetry except as an element connected to the rhythm, which is the remote survival of music in verse. And this rhythm, when it is perfect, ought to arise from the idea rather than from the word. A perfectly-conceived idea is rhythmical in itself; words that are spoken have not power to cheapen it. They can be hard and cool; it won't oppress; the words are unique and therefore the best. And being the best, they are the most beautiful.

April 9, 1930

29

f. Identity

... And so, in order to feel oneself being purely Oneself, each must be in relationship with all—absolutely all—other beings, and with each in the most profound relationship possible. Now, the most profound relationship possible is that of identity. Therefore, in order to feel oneself being purely Oneself, each must feel itself being all the others, absolutely consubstantiated with all the others.

There is no criterion for truth if not in agreeing with oneself. The universe doesn't agree with itself because it passes. Life doesn't agree with itself because it dies. Paradox is the typical formula of Nature. That's why all truth has a paradoxical form.

1924

✖ On Sensationism

1. The New Renaissance

For the Renaissance, Reality was Soul; for the Romantics, Reality was Nature. Now then, as our knowledge cannot exceed the limits of Soul and Nature, the New Renaissance (let's call it that) has no other basis for Reality. Its originality will derive therefore from its being a fusion of the Renaissance psyche with that of Romanticism.

There is no other conceivable hypothesis.

This fusion, however, produces a curious fact—the coexistence of two feelings about Reality, a double notion of Reality. But one can only have a notion of *one* Reality; Reality is only conceivable as *one*. The result, then, is that for the New Renaissance there must be a *fusion of Nature and Soul*. Reality will thus be *Nature-Soul*. That is, for the New Renaissance, *Nature will be understood as Soul*.

How, then, can the Real manifest itself as an irreality? For the irreal to be irreal it is necessary that it be real; therefore the Visible is an *irreal reality*, or a *real reality*—a realized contradiction. The Transcendent, then, is and is not at the same time; it exists beyond and not beyond its manifestation; it is real and not real in this manifestation. It is clear that this system is not materialism or spiritualism but a transcendent pantheism; let us call it then transcendental pantheism. There is only one eternal example of it. That is the cathedral of thought in Hegel's philosophy.

The transcendental pantheist involves and transcends all systems: Matter and spirit are simultaneously real and unreal for him, God and non-God essentially. It is just as true to say that matter and spirit exist as it is to say that they don't exist, because they exist and they don't exist at the same time. The ultimate truth one can say of a thing is that it exists and doesn't exist at the same time. Therefore, the essence of the universe is contradiction—the irrealization of the Real which is the realization of the Irreal—an affirmation that grows truer as it entails more. To say that matter is material and spirit spiritual is not false, but it is more true to say that matter is spiritual and spirit, material.

1914

2. Letter to an English Editor

Sir,

The purpose of this letter is to inquire whether you would be disposed to publish an anthology of Portuguese "sensationist" poetry. I am aware of how enterprising you are in this case of new "movements," and this emboldens me to make this inquiry. . . .

It is possibly not very easy to explain, in such a number of words as may legitimately be contained in a letter, precisely what the movement called sensationism is. I will try, however, to give you some idea of its nature; the extracts which I am enclosing, and which are translations of sensationist poems and parts of poems, will probably fill in the inevitable blanks of this cursory explanation.

First, as to derivation. It would be idle to pretend of Sensationism that is comes direct from the Gods or dates only from the souls of its creators without the human concourse of forerunners or influences. But we claim for it that it is as original as any human movement—intellectual or other—can be. That it does represent, both fundamentally (in its metaphysical substance) and superficially (in its innovations as to expression) a new species of *Weltanschauung,* we have no hesitation in claiming. As [I am] (I will not say [its] founder, for these things must never be said) [. . .] at least chief[ly] responsible for it, I owe it both to myself and to my fellow sinners to be no more modest over the matter than social usages absolutely require.

As to derivation, then; the enumeration of our origins will be the first element toward anything like an integral explanation of the movement. We descend from three older movements—French "symbolism," Portuguese transcendentalist pantheism, and the jumble of senseless and contradictory things of which futurism, cubism, and the like are occasional expressions; though, to be exact, we descend more from the spirit than from the letter of these. You know what French symbolism is and are of course aware that being at bottom a carrying-to-extremes of romantic subjectivism, it is besides a carrying-to-extremes of romantic liberty of versification. It was further an extremely minute and morbid analysis (synthesized for the purposes of poetical expression) of sensations. It was a "sensationism" already, though a rudimentary one, in relation to ours. It threw the world out of focus in obedience to those mental states the expression of which would have been incompatible with the normal equilibrium (balance) of sensations.

From French symbolism we derive our fundamental attitude of excessive attention to our sensations, our consequent frequent dealing in ennui, in apathy, in renouncement before the simplest and sanest things of life. This does not characterize all of us, though the morbid and probing analysis of sensations runs through the whole movement.

Now, as to the differences: We reject entirely, except occasionally for purely aesthetical purposes, the religious attitude of the symbolists. *God* has become for us a word which can conveniently be used for the suggestion of mystery, but which serves no other purpose moral or otherwise—an aesthetic value and no more. Besides this, we reject and abominate the symbolists' incapacity for prolonged effort, their inability to write long poems, and their vitiated "construction."

Portuguese "transcendentalist pantheism" you do not know. It is a pity because, though not a long-standing movement, [. . .] it is an original one. Suppose English romanticism had, instead of retrograding to the Tennysonian-Rossetti-Browning level, progressed right onward from Shelley, spiritualizing his already spiritualistic pantheism. You would arrive at the conception of Nature (our transcendentalist pantheists are essentially poets of Nature) in which flesh and spirit are entirely mingled in something which transcends both. If you can conceive a William Blake put into the soul of Shelley and writing through that, you will perhaps have a nearer idea of what I mean. This movement has produced two poems which I am bound to hold among the greatest of all time. Neither is a long one. One is the "Ode to Light" of Guerra Junqueiro, the greatest of all Portuguese poets (he drove Camoens from the first place when he published "Patria" in 1896, but "Patria," which is a lyrical and satirical drama, is not of his transcendental-pantheist phase). The "Prayer to Light" is probably the greatest metaphysico-poetical achievement since Wordsworth's great "Ode." The other poem, which certainly transcends Browning's "Last Ride Together" as a love poem, and which belongs to the same metaphysical level of love-emotion, though more religiously pantheistic, is the "Elegy" of Teixeira de Pascoaes, who wrote it in 1905. To this school of poets we, the "sensationists," owe the [way in which] spirit and matter are interpenetrated and intertranscended in our poetry. And we have carried the process further than the originators, though I regret to say that we cannot as yet claim to have produced anything on the level of the two poems I have referred to.

As to our influences from the modern movement [that] embraces cubism and futurism, [we are indebted] to the suggestions we received from them [rather] than to the substance of their works, properly speaking.

We have intellectualized their processes. The decomposition of the model they realize (because we have been influenced, not by their literature, if they have anything resembling literature, but by their pictures) we have carried into what we believe to be the proper sphere of that decomposition—not things, but our sensations of things.

Having shown you our origins, and, cursorily, our use of and differences from those origins, I will now state more expressly, as far as that is possible, in a few words, [. . .]the central attitude of Sensationism.

1. The only reality in life is sensation. The only reality in art is consciousness of [. . .] sensation.

2. There is no philosophy, no ethics, and even no aesthetics in art, whatever there may be in life. In art there are only sensations

and our consciousness of them. Whatever love, joy, pain, may be in life, in art they are only sensations; in themselves, they are worthless to art. God is a sensation of ours (because an idea is a sensation) and in art is used only in the expression of certain sensations, such as reverence, mystery, etcetera. No artist can believe or disbelieve in God, just as no artist can feel or not feel love or joy or pain. At the moment he writes, he either believes or disbelieves, according to the thought that best enables him to obtain consciousness and give expression to his sensation at that moment. Once that sensation goes, these things become to him, as artist, no more than bodies which the souls of sensations assume to become visible to that inner eye from whose sight he writes down his sensations.

3. Art, fully defined, is the harmonic expression of our consciousness of sensations; that is to say, our sensations must be so expressed that they create an object which will be a sensation to others. Art is not, as Bacon said, "man added to Nature"; it is sensation multiplied by consciousness—multiplied, be it well noted.

4. The three principles of art are (1) every sensation should be expressed to the full; that is, the consciousness of every sensation should be sifted to the bottom; (2) the sensation should be so expressed that it has the possibility of evoking—as a halo round a definite central presentation—the greatest possible number of other sensations; (3) the whole thus produced should have the greatest possible resemblance to an organized being, because that is the condition of vitality. I call these three principles Sensation, Suggestion, and Construction. This last—the great principle of the Greeks, whose great philosopher did indeed hold the poem to be "an animal"—has had very careless handling at modern hands. Romanticism has indisciplined the capacity of constructing which, at least, low classicism had. Shakespeare, with his fatal incapacity to visualize organized wholes, has been a fatal influence in this respect (you will remember that Matthew Arnold's classical instinct guided him to an intuition of this). Milton is still the great Master of Building in poetry. Personally, I confess that I tend ever more and more to put Milton above Shakespeare as a poet. But I must confess, insofar as I am anything (and I try hard not to be the same thing three minutes running because that is bad aesthetic hygiene), I am a pagan, and I

am therefore rather with the pagan artist Milton than with the Christian artist Shakespeare. All this, however, is passim, and I hope you will excuse its insertion in this place.

I sometimes hold that a poem—I would also say a painting or a statue, but I do not consider sculpture and painting arts, but only artisans' work—is a person, a living human being, [and] belongs in bodily presence and real fleshly existence to another world, into which our imagination throws him, his aspect, as we read him in this world being no more to us than the imperfect shadow of that reality of beauty which is divine elsewhere. I hope some day, after death, I shall meet in their real presences the few children of these I have as yet created, and I hope I shall find them beautiful in their dewy immortality. You may perhaps wonder that one who declares himself a pagan should subscribe to these imaginations. I was a pagan, however, two paragraphs above. I am one no longer as I write this. At the end of this letter I hope to be already something else. I carry into practice as far as I can that spiritual disintegration I preach. If I am ever coherent, it is only as an incoherence from incoherence. [. . .]

1916

3. Preface for an Anthology of Sensationist Poets *by Álvaro de Campos*

Sensationism began with the friendship between Fernando Pessoa and Mário de Sá-Carneiro. It is probably difficult to separate the part each of them had in the origin of the movement, and certainly quite useless to determine it. The fact is they built up the beginnings between them.

But each Sensationist worth mentioning is a separate personality, and they have naturally all interacted.

Fernando Pessoa and Mário de Sá-Carneiro stand nearest to the symbolists. Álvaro de Campos and Almada-Negreiros are the nearest to the more modern style of feeling and writing. The others are intermediate.

36

Fernando Pessoa suffers from classical culture.... His power lies more in the intellectual analysis of feeling and emotion, which he has carried to a perfection which renders us almost breathless. Of his static drama *The Sailor*, a reader once said, "It makes the exterior world quite unreal," and it does. No more remote thing exists in literature. Maeterlinck's best nebulosity and subtlety is coarse and carnal by comparison.

How [much] more interesting than the cubists and the futurists!

I never wished to know personally any of the sensationists, being persuaded that the best knowledge is impersonal.

Álvaro de Campos is excellently defined as a Walt Whitman with a Greek poet inside. He has all the power of intellectual, emotional, and physical sensation that characterized Whitman. But he has the precisely opposite trait—a power of construction and orderly development of a poem that no poet since Milton has attained. Álvaro de Campos's "Triumphal Ode," which is written in the Whitmanesque absence of stanza and rhyme (and regularity), has a construction and an orderly development which stultifies the perfection that *Lycidas,* for instance, can claim in this particular. "Naval [Maritime?] Ode," which covers no less than twenty-two pages of *Orpheu,* is a very marvel of organization. No German regiment ever had the inner discipline which underlies that composition, which, from its typographical aspect, might almost be considered ... a specimen of futurist carelessness. The same considerations apply to the magnificent "Salutation to Walt Whitman" in the third *Orpheu.*

The Portuguese sensationists are original and interesting because, being strictly Portuguese, they are cosmopolitan and universal. The Portuguese temperament is universal; that is its magnificent superiority. The one great act of Portuguese history, that long, cautious, scientific period of the Discoveries, is the one great cosmopolitan act in history. The whole people stamp themselves there. An original, typically Portuguese literature cannot be Portuguese because the typical Portuguese are never Portuguese. There is something American, with the noise left out and the quotidian omitted, in the intellectual temper of this people. No people seizes so readily on novelties. No people depersonalizes so magnificently. That weakness is its great strength. That temperamental nonregionalism is its unused might. That indefiniteness of soul is what makes [the Portuguese people] definite.

Sep. / Oct. 1916

4. Notes on Sensationism

There is nothing, no reality, but sensation. Ideas are sensations, but of things not placed in space and sometimes not even in time.

Logic, the place of ideas, is another kind of space.

Dreams are sensations with only two dimensions. Ideas are sensations with only one dimension. A line is an idea.

Every sensation (of a solid thing) is a solid body bounded by planes, which are *inner images* (of the nature of dreams—two-dimensioned), bounded themselves by lines (which are *ideas,* of one dimension only). *Sensationism pretends, taking stock of this real reality, to realize in art a decomposition of reality into its psychic geometrical elements.*

The end of art is simply to increase human self-consciousness. Its criterion is general (or semigeneral) acceptance, sooner or later, for that is the proof that it does tend to increase self-consciousness in men.

The more we decompose and analyze into their psychic elements our sensations, the more we increase our self-consciousness. Art has, then, the duty of becoming increasingly conscious. In the classic age, art developed consciousness on the level of the three-dimensional sensation, that is, art applied itself to a perfect and clear visioning of reality [taken to be] solid. Hence the Greek mental attitude, which seems so strange to us, of introducing concepts such as that of the sphere into the most abstract abstractions, as in the case of Parmenides, whose idealistic conception of a highly abstract universe yet admits of a description of it as spherical.

Post-Christian art has worked constantly toward the creating of a two-dimensional art.

We must create a one-dimensional art.

38

This seems a narrowing of art, and to a certain extent it is.

Cubism, futurism, and kindred schools are wrong applications of intuitions that are fundamentally right. The wrong lies in the fact that they attempt to solve the problem they suspect on the lines of three-dimensional art; their fundamental error lies in that they attribute to sensations an exterior reality, which indeed they have, but not in the sense the futurists and others believe. The futurists are something absurd, like Greeks trying to be modern and analytic.

1916

Sensationism differs from common literary currents in that it is not exclusive, that is to say, it does not claim for itself the monopoly of right aesthetic feeling. Properly speaking, it does not claim for itself that it is, except in a certain restricted sense, a current or a movement, but only partly an attitude and partly an addition to all preceding currents.

The position of sensationism is not as [in] common literary movements [like] romanticism, symbolism, futurism, and others, a position analogous to that of a religion, which implicitly excludes other religions. It is precisely analogous to that which theosophy takes up in respect to all religious systems. It is a well-known fact that theosophy claims to be, not a religion, but the fundamental truth that underlies all religious systems alike. As such, theosophy is in opposition, of course, to those parts of religious systems that exclude other systems and also to those parts of religious systems that seem to it to vitiate the fundamental attitude called religious. That is why theosophy, while it does not oppose protestantism as such, opposes it insofar as it is opposed to catholicism, and why it cannot accept such theories as that of eternal penalties, which vitiate, in its opinion, all that is fundamental and true in the sense of the worship of God's creation.

Even so, the position of sensationism is relative to all artistic movements. It holds that all or almost all of them (for we must not allow this term "artistic movements" to be applicable with a universal generosity to every snake that raises its head above that of others in the literary pitcher of modern confusion) are, in their

39

essence, right. Spinoza said that philosophical systems are right in what they affirm and wrong in what they deny. This, the greatest of all pantheistic affirmations, is what sensationism can repeat in relation to aesthetic things. Though supreme perfection (which is unattainable) is only one, [. . .] relative perfection is several. Homer is as perfect in his way as Herrick in his, although the Homeric way is a far superior one. The sensationist admits joyfully both Homer and Herrick to the great brotherhood of Art.

There are three central tenets of sensationism. The first is that art is supremely construction and that the greatest art is that which is able to visualize and create organized wholes, of which the component parts fit *vitally* into their places: the great principle that Aristotle enunciated when he said that a poem was an "animal." The second is that, all art being composed of parts, each of those parts must be perfect in itself. As the [first tenet is] the classic principle of unity and structural perfection, this [second one] is the romantic principle of "fine passages" [that would make those sufficient for] what they contain of truth, and exclude the error that makes of all this, without attending to the higher classical principle that the whole is greater than the part. The third tenet of sensationism, qua aesthetics, is that every little fragment which builds up the part of the whole should be perfect in itself; this is the principle that is insisted on to exaggeration by all those artists of which the symbolists are part, who, being temperamentally incapable of creating either great organized wholes or even (as the Romantics) large eloquent stretches, put their activity into the eggshell (nutshell) of producing beautiful individual lines or very short perfect lyrics. That is beautiful indeed, when it is beautiful, but it is dangerous to fall under the impression that that is anything but the lowest part of art.

These are the tenets of sensationism qua artistic philosophy. That is to say, these are the tenets it upholds insofar as it accepts all systems and schools of art, extracting from each that beauty and originality which is peculiar to it.

Sensationism stands for the aesthetic attitude in all its pagan splendor. It does not stand for any of those foolish things— the aestheticism of Oscar Wilde, or the art for art's sake of other misguided people with a plebeian outlook on life. It can see the loveliness of morals just as it can understand the beauty of the lack of them. No religion is right for it, nor any religion wrong.

A man may traverse all the religious systems of the world in one day with perfect sincerity and tragic soul-experiences. He must be an aristocrat—in the sense in which we use the word—to be able to do it. I once stated that a cultured and intelligent man has the duty to be an atheist at noon, when the clearness and materiality of the sun eats into all things, and an ultramontane catholic at that precise hour after sunset when the shadows have not yet completed their slow coil round the clear presence of things. Some people thought that this was a joke. But I was only translating into rapid prose (this was written in a newspaper) a common personal experience. Having accustomed myself to have no beliefs and no opinions lest my aesthetic feeling should be weakened, I grew soon to have no personality at all except an expressive one. I grew to be a mere apt machine for the expression of moods that became so intense that they grew into personalities and made my very soul the mere shell of their casual appearance, even as theosophists say that the malice of nature-spirits sometimes makes them occupy the discarded astral corpses of men and frolic under cover of their shadowy semblances (substances).

This does not mean that every sensationist should have no political opinion; it means that, as artist, he is bound to have none and all. That excuse of Martial's, which has roused the ire of many people alien to the essence of art—"Lasciva est nobis pagina, vita proba"—that though his art was impure, his life was not (reproduced later by Herrick, who wrote of himself, "His muse was jocund, but his life was chaste"), is the exact duty of the artist toward himself.

Sincerity is the one great artistic crime. Insincerity is the second greatest. The great artist should never have a really fundamental and sincere opinion about life. But that should give him the capacity to feel sincere, nay, to be absolutely sincere about anything for a certain length of time—that length of time, say, which is necessary for a poem to be conceived and written. It is perhaps necessary to state that it is necessary to be an artist before this can be

41

attempted. It is of no use to try to be an aristocrat when you are a born middle-class man or plebeian.

1916

5. [To feel is to create]

To feel is to create.

To feel is to think without ideas, and therefore, feeling is understanding, given that the Universe has no ideas.

But what is feeling?

Holding opinions is not feeling.

All our opinions are others'.

Thinking is wanting to transmit to others that which one believes one feels.

Only what is thought can be communicated to others. What is felt is incommunicable. Only the *value* of what we feel can be communicated. We can only make one feel what we feel. Not that the reader feels the same pain(?). It is enough that the reader feels in the same way.

Feeling opens the doors of the prison in which thought locks the soul.

Lucidity should only reach the threshold of the soul. In the very antechambers of feeling it is forbidden to be explicit.

Feeling is understanding. Thinking is going wrong. To understand what another person thinks is to disagree with that person. To understand what that person feels is to be that person. Being another person is of great metaphysical value. God is all people.

To see, hear, smell, to have a hankering to touch—these are the sole commandments of God. Feelings are divine because they are our relationship with the Universe, and our relationship with Universe-God.

There is no criterion for truth if it is not in not agreeing with oneself. The universe doesn't agree with itself because it passes. Life doesn't agree with itself because it dies. Paradox is the typical formula of Nature. That's why all truth has a paradoxical form. . . . To affirm is to deceive oneself at the threshold. To think is to limit. To reason means to exclude. There is much it is good to think about because there is much it is good to limit and exclude.

Substitute yourself always. You are not enough for yourself. Be unpredictable always for yourself. Let yourself happen before yourself. Let your sensations be purely accidental, adventures that happen to you. You must be a universe without laws in order to be superior.

These are the principles of sensationism. . . .

Make of your soul a metaphysics, an ethics, and an aesthetics. Substitute yourself with God casually. It is the only truly religious attitude. (God is everywhere except within himself.)

Make of your being an atheistic religion and of your sensations a ritual and a cult. . . .

✖ Literature and the Artist

1. Celebrity and Art

I [propose] to examine the problem of celebrity, both occasional and permanent; to investigate in what conditions either sort has happened to men; and to foresee, as far as can be, in what conditions either sort is likely to happen in the future. Celebrity is the acceptance of any man or of any group of men as in some way valuable to mankind. To investigate the problem, we shall have to define celebrity. We shall also have to define mankind.

1. Celebrity may be of things or of men. There are celebrated crimes, battles, novels; there are celebrated authors of these. We shall not concern ourselves with the things, but with the men. It is the conditions that produce celebrity that interest us.

2. Celebrity may be incidental or fundamental. A man who is killed in a particularly mysterious manner becomes celebrated by his death. If the case is important, he may be immortal through history as an interesting corpse. We are not interested in incidental but in fundamental celebrity, however unjust it may happen to be.

3. Celebrity may be artificial and natural. A king is naturally famous. He is born into [it] with the kingdom. We shall not concern ourselves with this sort of celebrity. It varies with manners and customs, with institutions. We shall examine only the problem of artificial celebrity.

4. Celebrity may be good or bad; the second sort being generally called notoriety. The shifting ideas of good and evil sometimes complicate the problem; they are even superimposed in some cases. Where one sees a murderer, another will see a bold man. Where one sees a martyr, another will see a fool. The

45

difficulty of the point has been [made], with no intention of [making] it, in Proudhon's famous phrase: "After the tyrants, I know nothing more hateful than the martyrs."

1925

2. Genius and the Times

Genius is insanity made sane by dilution in the abstract, like a poison converted into a medicine by mixture. Its proper product is abstract novelty—that is to say, a novelty that conforms at bottom to the general laws of human intelligence and not to the particular laws of mental disease. The essence of genius is inadaptation to environment; that is why genius (unless it be accompanied by talent or wit) is generally uncomprehended [in] its environment; and I say "generally" and not "universally" because much depends on the environment. It is not the same thing to be a genius in ancient Greece and in modern Europe or the modern world.

Shakespeare was unknown as a genius in his time, for the loud though posthumous praises of Ben Jonson are no more than the loud language of the time, devoid of meaning and applied by the same Jonson to men of whom no one today knows anything— [such as] Lord Mounteagle, of whom he says that he "stood the master-mind" (no less) in that time, or the very James I.

Shakespeare was admired in his time as a wit, not as a man of genius. How could he be admired as a man of genius? It was the creator of Falstaff that could be understood; the creator of Hamlet could not be. If the anti-Stratfordians [greges] had ever taken the trouble to notice this, many absurd comparisons with the praise given to Jonson or to other men of their time would have been rendered impossible.

Shakespeare is the example of great genius and great wit linked to insufficiency of talent. He is as supreme in the intuition that constitutes genius and in the quickness of strangeness that constitutes wit as he is deficient in the constructiveness and the coordination which constitute talent.

46

3. [The pressure of a known name]

If anyone wishes clearly to understand what is meant by the pressure of a known name, he need but figure to himself the following hypothesis. Let him suppose a book of poems, published today, by an unknown poet. Let that book be composed of great poems of great poets. Let it be submitted, in the course of reviewing, to a competent critic who, by some odd chance, might happen to be ignorant of every poem there printed, even though acquainted with every poet represented. Does anyone suppose that the competent critic, even if he had it in his power to write, say, the leading article in *The Times Literary Supplement* (no less would be deserved by such a book), would write anything more than a short notice, in 6-point type, in the bibliographical part of that paper? And the poet would be lucky if he got a notice in the text pages.

The pressure of a known name does not mean that the critic will think a poem good or bad in function [because] of a known name. But he will give careful attention, word by word and phrase by phrase, to the poem of a reputed poet; he will do nothing of the sort [for] the absolute stranger. If anyone will take the trouble, as I once did, either to pass off as the work of an unknown poet, or of his own self (this was what I did), the poem of a celebrated poet; or if he will pass off some unknown lines as [those of] a celebrated poet, he will discover this very easily. In both cases and for opposite reasons the lines must be good or the test will not be just. . . .

4. Art and Ideas

It is ideas, as distinct from purposes, that make immortality—ideas as form and not as substance. In art everything is form, and everything includes ideas. It does not matter to the judgment of posterity whether a poem contains materialist or idealist notions; it matters whether these notions are high or not, agreeable in their form—even their mental and abstract form—or disagreeable.

This would seem to make propaganda not injurious to art, so long as there is art. It is indeed not essentially injurious, but, that

47

it may not so be, it is necessary that, against his own purpose and intent, the artist forget the propaganda in the art. It may be that the *Divine Comedy* is intended to be Catholic propaganda—a rather futile thing in Catholic times; but Dante, when he wrote it, forgot all about the propaganda and wrote poetry. The propaganda does no harm to the poetry for the simple reason that it did not get there. The result is that a third of Dante's commentators consider the *Divine Comedy* heretical, and many of these [consider it] as purposely so. If the poem can be considered as Catholic and anti-Catholic, the propaganda is certainly not very efficacious. The same applies to the kindred and different poem which stands beside the *Divine Comedy* on the sorting of [i.e. as determined by] the ages. Milton wrote it down as his purpose to justify the ways of God to man, and his poem contains two heroes—Satan, who revolts against God, and Adam, whom God has punished. [Milton] has justified the ways of man to God. His poem is set up [as] an epic for one form of Christianity, and the result is that the author was an Arian, his form of Christianity being the absence of Christianity. (With his vast learning and experience of the learned, he has put everything into his Christian epic; the only thing left out was Christ. Has anyone ever felt Christian after reading *Paradise Lost?*

5. Morality and Art

This problem of immoral art is one that is ever cropping up, centering for the moment round one work or another, which puts the vague principles involved in that problem into public focus.

... We will take [up] the problem as [it] ... concerns ... literature. The only classification admissible in literature that concerns this problem ... [involves] literature proper and mere obscene writing. That obscene writing, which is the script-equivalent of, say, obscene photographs in which the only possible justification is obscenity, belongs palpably to a different species than the writing that is literary and in which either obscene elements are superimposed on the literary substructure or inextricably interwoven with the artistic substance thereof. So that, if authorities are to interfere in this problem, they have to proceed, first, on a palpably aesthetic basis.

The question, as all questions, is of degrees. There are works which are palpably only obscene and not literary at all, such as those pamphlets we have just named, which correspond in written manner to the obscene photographs that we also cited [as a] parallel. And there are, at the other end, products such as *Venus and Adonis,* like so many classical poems and prose works; the difficulty is greatest when we meet with high works of art which are not only immoral but frankly apologetic for some species of immorality.

It cannot be claimed that the artistic elements involved absolve and extirpate the immorality of the work. Of the two kinds of public that read, the lower one does not see the artistic elements and enters into the significance of only the immoral elements contained in the work of art. The other portion of the reading public, that portion which is sensitive to artistic influences and able therefore to effect a separation between the two kinds of elements which are, by hypothesis, involved in the kind of artistic work we are discussing, is not very far from the other public in reference to effects; for, if the work be really a high work of art, and the immoral elements therefore not foreign to the substance of it but inextricably wound up with it, these immoral elements are brought all the more into prominence, inasmuch as they gain intensity, beauty, and fervor through the artistic way they are put.

Venus and Adonis is very likely to excite sexual feelings in a feebly educated person; but it is, if anything, still more likely to excite them in a highly educated or highly sensitive one. The very artistic superiority of the work ensures that effect. The principle that "to the pure all things are pure" is pure fireworks; there are no "pure."

If we wish to prohibit the sale of immoral art, we cannot do so without prohibiting art at the same time. The problem is especially difficult when we have to consider nonextreme works, that is, works that are not palpably superior from the artistic standpoint, but ... also are not pure obscenity, mere obscenity and no more. When we are at the Shakespeare level, we all more or less agree that it would be tantamount to violence to prohibit the circulation of immoral literature. When we are at the literary level correspondent to the obscene photograph, only the traders in it will not agree to its suppression. But when we are [... at] the popular novelist level, the problem becomes very difficult. To a certain extent works on a literary par with Mr. Hall Caine's or Miss Marie Corelli's are literature; though they are [not lasting] literature— though several people, indeed, might claim for them a superior level. If such works convey obscenity or immorality, what is to be done to them?

The central fact is that the problem is elsewhere and its solution rendered impossible until we decide to see that some classification of publics must be entered into before any light at all breaks into the discussion.

For the essential difference between the uneducated and the educated reading of, say, *Venus and Adonis* is that, though both educated and uneducated are very possibly sensually excited to the same degree while reading the work, the after-influence differs; special cases and morbid ones being, of course, not considered. A little after finishing *Venus and Adonis,* the uneducated reader who has not been bored but kept interested by the sexual part of it, remains under the influence of that part of it which interested him, and that is the sexual one. Whereas the educated reader, once past the momentary excitement of the work, remains rather under the influence of the artistic elements.

The second distinction to be effected is between adult and nonadult public. An adult is held to be one who is able to shift for himself, which a child is not. So that, in this field, the problem becomes simple: The reading of immoral works, of whatever kind they be, should be forbidden to children but permitted to adults.

Among adults, the distinction follows: There are the educated and the uneducated ones, and the latter are, to a certain extent, in the position of children. So that, if prohibition is to some extent to be decided on, it should be extensive only to the uneducated part of the public. The question of how that is to be effected is quite secondary and solvable, if only approximately, in several ways.

1914

6. The Uselessness of Criticism

That good work always comes to the fore is a worthless affirmation if it apply to really good work and [if] by "coming to the fore" it refer to acceptance in its own time. That good work always comes to the fore on the course of its futurity is true; that second-rate good work always comes to the fore in its own age is also true.

For how is a critic to judge? What are the qualities that make not the casual but the competent critic? A knowledge of past art or literature, a taste refined by that knowledge, and an impartial and judicious spirit. Anything less than that is fatal to the true play of the critical faculties. Anything more than that is already creative spirit, and therefore individuality; and individuality means self-centeredness and a certain imperviousness to the work of others.

How competent, however, is the competent critic? Let us suppose a deeply original work of art comes before his eyes. How does he judge it? By comparison with the works of art of the past. If it be original, however, it will depart in something—and the more original, the more it will depart from the works of art of the past. Insofar as it does this, it will seem not to conform to the aesthetic canon that the critic finds established in his mind. And if its originality, instead of lying in a departure from those old standards, lie in a use of them on more severely constructive lines—as Milton used the ancients—will the critic take that bettering to be a bettering, or the use of those standards to be an imitation? Will he rather see the builder than the user of the building materials? Why should he rather do one thing than the better one? Of all elements, constructiveness is the most difficult to determine in a work. . . . A fusion of past elements—will the critic see this fusion of . . . elements?

Does anyone persuade himself that if *Paradise Lost* were published today, or *Hamlet,* or Shakespeare's or Milton's sonnets, they would be rated above Mr. Kipling's poetry, or Mr. Noyes's, or that of any other similarly quotidian gentleman? If anyone persuades himself of that, he is a fool. The expression is short, not sweet, but it is meant only to be true.

On every side we hear the cry that the age needs a great poet. The central hollowness of all modern achievement is a thing rather felt than spoken about. If the great poet were to appear, who would be there to notice him? Who can say whether he has not already appeared? The reading public sees in the papers notices of the work of those men whose influence and friendships have made them known, or whose secondariness has made them accepted [by] the crowd. The great poet may have appeared already; his work will have been noticed in a few *vient de paraître* words in some bibliographic summary of a critical paper.

7. The Art of Representation

The basis of acting is misrepresentation. The art of the actor consists in employing the author's drama in showing his acting ability upon it. The piece is like a bar whereon the actor shows his gymnastic abilities. He is only limited by the necessary conditions of a bar; he can do only a limited number of things with it, but those he can do in a thousand individual ways.

Acting, again, has all the attraction of forgery. We all love a forger. It is a very human and a quite instinctive sentiment. We all adore trickery and counterfeit. Acting unites and intensifies, through the material and vital character of its manifestations, all the low instincts of the artistic instinct—the riddle instinct, the trapeze instinct, the prostitute instinct. It is popular and appreciated for these reasons, or, rather, for this reason.

The artist's thirst for glory is made flesh in the actor's thirst for applause. All appearance before people is low. All assemblies are crowds and, if not sweaty in body, at least sweaty in emotions.

All coarse minds adore speech. To be wordy is itself vulgar. The only thing that renders wordiness interesting is profanity and obscenity, for these things are "in character" therewith. Wordiness without dirty words and coarse phrases is feminine and therefore vulgar.

8. The Artist and Emotion

Anyone who is in any way a poet knows very well how much easier it is to write a good poem (if good poems lie in the man's power) about a woman who interests him very much than about a woman he is deeply in love with. The best sort of love poem is generally written about an abstract woman.

A great emotion is too selfish; it takes into itself all the blood of the spirit, and the congestion leaves the hands too cold to write. Three sorts of emotions produce great poetry—strong but quick emotions, seized upon for art as soon as they have passed, but not before they have passed; strong and deep emotions in their remembrance a long time after; and false emotions, that is to say, emotions felt in the intellect. Not insincerity, yet a translated sincerity, is the basis of all art.

The great general who would win a battle for the empire of his country and the history of his people does not wish—he cannot wish—to have many of his soldiers slain. Yet, once he has entered into the contemplation of his strategy, he will choose (without a thought of his men) the better stroke, though it lose him a hundred thousand men, rather than the worse or even . . . the slower action, which may leave him nine-tenths of those men he fights with and for and whom he generally loves. He becomes an artist for the sake of his fellow countrymen, and he mows down his fellow countrymen for their strategical sake.

He (the artist) may not be intelligent, but he must be intellectual.

Art is the intellectualization of sensation (feeling) through expression. The intellectualization is given in, by, and through the expression itself. That is why great artists—even great artists in literature, which is the most intellectual of the arts—are so often unintelligent persons.

A Greek intellect and a modern sensibility. A Greek intellect: even if we suppose that a Greek intellect does not mean an eternal intellect, still the Greek discipline of thought is the

53

scientific basis of all art. A modern sensibility: we cannot maim our emotions to please.

Yet our discipline, though Greek in quality, cannot be Greek in quantity. Our sensibility is of complexities that antiquity could not even dream of; so our discipline of that sensibility must involve the use of a far higher quantum of intellectual force.

The Greeks might have felt deeply or strongly or wildly, but they always felt rationally. Their emotions were born reasonable, even when born fiery and violent. Not only can we not attain to that quality, but we must not; for, if we had the Greek intellect and the Greek feeling, we would be ancient Greeks, not modern Europeans.

1915

9. The Art of Translating Poetry

A poem is an intellectualized impression, or an idea made emotion, communicated to others by means of a rhythm. This rhythm is double-in-one, like the concave and convex aspects of the same arch; it is made up of a verbal or musical rhythm and of a visual or image rhythm that . . . [corresponds to it internally].

The translation of a poem should therefore [conform] absolutely (1) to the idea or emotion that constitutes the poem, (2) to the verbal rhythm in which that idea or emotion is expressed; it should conform relatively to the inner or visual rhythm, keeping the images themselves when it can, but keeping always to the type of image.

It was on this criterion that I based my translations into Portuguese of Poe's "Annabel Lee" and "Ulalume," which I translated, not because of their great intrinsic worth, but because they were a standing challenge to translators.

10. An Essay on Drama (excerpt)

The pertinent cultural phenomena that distinguish our age from others are, first, in the field of general culture, the extension, compulsion, and intensity of scientific culture; secondly, in the field restricted to artistic culture since Romanticism, the tendency to substitute the processes of suggestion for those of definition in the accomplishment of the work; thirdly, in the even more restricted field of theatrical culture, the special improvements of the scenic impulse and of the art of performance.

11. Shakespeare

The basis of lyrical genius is hysteria. The more pure and narrow the lyrical genius, the clearer the hysteria is, as in the cases of Byron and Shelley. But in this case the hysteria is, so to speak, physical; that is why it is clear.

In the lyrical genius of the grade above this—that which ranges over several types of emotion—the hysteria becomes, so to speak, mental; . . . because, as in Victor Hugo, a violent physical health drives it inward from physical manifestation.

In the lyrical genius of the highest grade—that which ranges over all types of emotion, incarnating them in persons and so perpetually depersonalizing itself—the hysteria becomes, so to speak, purely intellectual.

1928

Hysteria takes on different mental forms according to the general temperament with which it happens to coincide. If health be frail in any way, the form of hysteria will be almost physical; and, if the hysteric be a lyric poet, he will sing out of his emotions and, the greater number of times, out of a small number of emotions. If health be good or very good, the constitution strong, and, except for the hysteria, the nerves fairly sane, the operation of hysteria will be purely mental; then the lyric poet produced will be one who will sing of a variety of emotions without going out of himself—either because, like Goethe, who was of this type, he had a variety of emotions, all, however, personal, or because, like Victor Hugo, he was constantly, though uniformly and monotonously, impersonal and fictitious. If, finally, the constitution be neutral, that is to say, neither strong nor weak, as in the case of a frail but not unhealthy man, the operation of hysteria will become vaguely physical and vaguely mental, neither wholly one thing nor the other; the result will be, in the case of the lyric poet, a mixture of the two others— the capacity to *live* in imagination the mental states of hysteria, the power therefore to project them outward into separate persons. In other and more precise words, it is the psychological ability which goes to make, but does not essentially make, the dramatist.

(Shakespeare was then (1) by nature, and in youth and early manhood, a hysteric; (2) later, and in full manhood, a hystero-neurasthenic; (3) at the end of his life, a hystero-neurasthenic in a lesser degree; he was also of a frail constitution and of deficient vitality, but not unhealthy. Thus much we have determined already.)

Great as his tragedies are, none of them is greater than the tragedy of his own life. The gods gave him all great gifts but one; the one they gave not was the power to use those great gifts greatly. He stands forth as the greatest example of genius, pure genius, genius immortal and unavailing. His creative power was shattered into a thousand fragments by the stress and oppression of [such things.] It is but the shreds of itself. *Disjecta membra,* said Carlyle, are what we have of any poet, or of any man. Of no poet or man is this truer than of Shakespeare.

He stands before us, melancholy, witty, at times half insane, never losing his hold on the objective world, ever knowing what he wants, dreaming ever high purposes and impossible greatnesses, and waking ever to mean ends and low triumphs. This, this was his great experience of life; for there is no great experience of life that is not, finally, the calm experience of disillusion.

His wavering purpose; his unsettled will; his violent and fictitious emotions; his great, formless thoughts, his intuition, the greatest that has ever been, seeing right through a thought and expressing it as if the thought itself spoke, living an alien life down to its blood and flesh and speaking from it as the man himself could never have done; his power of observation, gathering a whole thing into one paramount aspect; his practical ability born of his quick understanding of things. . . .

When the higher faculties of the mind are broken, in abeyance, or sluggish in their operation, the lower ones assume an

56

unwonted force. Thus his practical ability was the one thing that withstood the stress and pressure of life and lack of will. He could amass money who strove in vain to amass the completion of created beauty.

He began with two long narrative poems—highly imperfect as narrative wholes, and that is the beginning of his secret—written when he had yet a greater instinct to write than the intellectual impulse for it. With broadening consciousness, he lost his rapidity.

Shakespeare was initially more vain than proud; at the end of his life—or at least of his writing life—he became more proud than vain. It is easy to conjecture why: He was unappreciated; what appreciation he had was more [an insult] than to be enjoyed; for whereas he was rated well, he was not rated high, and thinking and knowing himself (for this he must have done) the greatest genius of his age, he yet saw how whatever appreciation was shown him bulked small in view of the admiration in which Jonson was held, and others lesser than Jonson, and how appreciation no smaller than shown to him was shown to Daniel, to Webster, and who knows if even to the Mundays ("our best plotter"), the Heywoods, and the Days. His vanity was necessarily shaken by this, if not abolished altogether; and the tendency to depression, fatal in a temperament of which neurasthenia is a component, must have achieved the transformation.

Pride is the consciousness (right or wrong) of our own worth, vanity the consciousness (right or wrong) of the obviousness of our own worth to others. A man may be proud without being vain, he may be both vain and proud, he may be—for such is human nature—vain without being proud. It is at first sight difficult to understand how we can be conscious of the obviousness of our worth to others without the consciousness of our worth itself. If human nature were rational, there would be no explanation at all. Yet man lives first an outer, then an inner, life; notion of effect precedes, in the evolution of mind, the notion of the inner cause of effect. Man prefers being rated high for what he is not to being rated half-high for what he is. This is vanity's working.

57

As the universal qualities of mankind all exist in every man, in however low a degree of one or another, so [. . . each is] to some extent proud and to some extent vain.

Pride is, of itself, timid and contractive; vanity, bold and expansive. He who is sure (however wrongly) that he will win or conquer cannot fear. Fear—where it is not a morbid disposition rooted in neurosis—is no more than want of confidence in ourselves to overcome a danger.

When, therefore, Shakespeare's vanity gave way to pride, or, better, when the mixture of much vanity and some pride that was initial in him gave way to a mixture of scant vanity and some pride, he was automatically dulled for action, and the neurasthenic element of his character spread like a slow flood over the surface of his hysteria.

The outward intellectual sign of vanity is the tendency to mockery and the abasement of others. He only can mock and delight in the confusion of others who instinctively feels himself not amenable to similar mockery and abasement. The earlier part of Shakespeare's work is full of "gulls," of derision of some figures. He takes part with some of his creations against others. . . .

This declined toward the end of his written work. Humor supplanted wit. Humor is no more than the consciousness that what is laughable is akin to ourselves. It is born of the opposite of both vanity and pride, that is to say, of humility, of the sense, rational or instinctive, that at bottom we are no more than other men. Humor, if it had a philosophy, would be deterministic. The effect of the pride he had in checking his vanity, and the further checks on that vanity from unappreciation and [. . . a lack of] success in higher things, liberated Shakespeare's humor more and more.

His very pride could not grow because unappreciation dulls pride itself, if pride be not overweening and temperamental, as it was, for instance, in Milton, who, though not very vain, had nevertheless more vanity than he would have liked to have been aware of.

(Let us admire, yet never idolize. And if we must idolize, let us idolize truth only, for it is the only idolatry that cannot corrupt, since what idolatry corrupts is truth, and the idolatry of truth is therefore the only one which cannot corrupt.)

Only an overweening and temperamental pride can resist constant unappreciation; some doubt must creep into the mind as to whether its sense of its own worth is really valid. The introspective mind has so often seen its Junos turn out to be clouds that it cannot be shaken in the assurance of so naturally misleading a thing as a man's appreciation of himself.

Unappreciation. There are things in Shakespeare which a lower Elizabethan might have written in a happy moment; these were surely appreciated. But these are the lesser part of Shakespeare; if he had written but them, he would have been a man of talent, of great talent perhaps, not, as he essentially was, a man of genius. Insofar as he was not an Elizabethan poet but Shakespeare, that is to say, insofar as he was what we now admire him essentially for having been, he is sure to have been unappreciated. Those flashes of intuitive expression, which in a cluster of words gather the scents of a thousand springs, those sudden epithets that flash down into the abysses of understanding, these, which are our daily astonishment and the reading over of which cannot pall their novelty nor sear their freshness, must have fallen flat on contemporary minds, for it is in these that Shakespeare, like genius itself, was "above his age." How can an age understand or appreciate what is, by definition, above it? Much of the best he wrote will have been taken for rant, nonsense, or madness. We may rest assured that, if we could call up Jonson from the shades and ask him for examples of that [Shakespeare's] want of art (. . .), we would be surprised to hear him cite, among things which are perchance rant, many of the jewels of Shakespeare's greater verse.

Yet, as there is an intuition of understanding just as there is one of conception, one as rare and as flashlike as the other, once or twice some of the higher spirits of the age must have caught a sudden glimpse of his transcendence. This would be the worse for the appreciation of the author. Nothing so harms a man in the estimation of others as the sense that he may be their better. To the general and constant sense that he is not their superior there is added the occasional suspicion that he may be, and unappreciation, colorless in itself, takes on the hue of envy, for men envy by supposition who admire only under certainty. Hesitation as to whether a man may be our better is as unnerving as hesitation as to whether something disagreeable may happen to us; we hope not, but we hope uncertainly. And, as we thereby fear the more the event we half-fear, we, in the other case, dislike the more the man we almost admire. In both cases, we dread the possibility of certainty more than the certainty itself ("we know not if we must admire").

Whether it is only the sense of unappreciation that plays like a gloom over the darker tragedies of Shakespeare's maturity, it is impossible to ascertain, but it is not likely that such unappreciation should have stood alone in the causation of the melancholy that shows directly in *Hamlet,* that trickles through the phrases of *Othello* and *King Lear,* that, here and there, twists, as if following the contortion of the suffering mind, the very wording of the supreme expressions of *Antony and Cleopatra.* Unappreciation itself unfolds into several depressive elements. We have, first, unappreciation itself, secondly, the appreciation of lesser men, thirdly, the sense that some effort like that of other men—the learning of one, the connections of another, the chance, whatever it might have been, of a third—might have conquered the difficulty. But the very genius that causes the initial unappreciation dulls the mind to the activities that could counteract it. The poor and proud man, who knows that he would be less poor if he could but beg or humble himself, suffers no less from his poverty, not only from the better status of men less proud or more fortunate, but also from the impossibility of begging . . . or stooping as they do to what frees them from a similar poverty. There is then a revolt of the man against his own temperament; doubt sets in towards himself, and, as the poor and proud man may ask himself whether he is not rather unskilled in the things of practice than too proud to descend to them, or whether his pride be not the mask to himself of his incompetence for action, the unappreciated man of genius may fall into doubt whether his inferiority of practical sense is not an inferiority in itself and not only the negative side of a superiority, the defect or a merit which could not exist without that defect.

60

Shakespeare's case was patently worse. He had stooped to the same arts as the lesser men that stood higher than he, as the still lesser men that stood as high as he or very little below him. He had done the same hackwork as they, without having been worn [out by] ... that hackwork. He had altered and arranged alien plays, and (whatever he may have thought of that, for it is possible he may have impugned that less than we imagine, being both used to it and integrated in the environment of that activity), he surely cannot have adapted himself to those conditions to the insane extent of thinking he was thereby doing justice to his great genius or [being] in the right place of action for the possibilities of his mind. By doing what lesser men were naturally doing he had become himself, outwardly at least, a lesser man. Not only had he not revealed himself by thus stooping to the common drudgery; he had masked himself the more.

For the learning, which was part of Jonson's credit with the public, he had, as we have seen, neither appetence nor patience; possibly he even had not time; and he had not received it in early youth, when it is imposed and not sought. From the establishment of influential connections, a humble condition possibly, a lack of disposition certainly, debarred him. [As for] pushing his way among equals by the social craft of mutual praise and the like, the pride he had, though not great, was too great, and it would have grown against the attempt, and gathered a fictitious force in the misuse.

He had possibly triumphed and made his way materially, insofar as money was concerned. That also, though agreeable in itself—whatever its exact degree might have been—must have figured as an ironic comment in the margin of his unappreciation. To fail to be known justly as a poet is not compensated by just success as a shopkeeper.

Shakespeare is the greatest failure in literature, and it is perhaps not too much to suppose that he must have been, to a great extent, aware of it. That vigilant mind could not have deceived itself as to this. The tragedy of his unsuccess was but the greater [... in combination] with the comedy of his success.

All these are but modes and shapes of the unappreciation he felt. But the depression of spirit, the dulling of the will, the sickening of purpose, which the sense of unappreciation caused, must have made themselves felt on other lines than the direct work for which his mind felt itself born. The will that was dulled for writing must have been dulled also for other ways of action. The depression of spirit must have had outlets other than the figure of Hamlet and the phrasing of the greater tragedies. The sickening of purpose must have discolored his life, as it paled his poems and his plays. And the joys untasted, the activities uncared for, the tasks avoided and remitted must have recoiled, in their mental effect, upon the depression that engendered them and made greater the dispiritedness which was their cause.

To this extent we may justly and confidently go. What else there was, foreign to this, to eradicate that depression we cannot now determine—if there was anything. What outward events of an untoward nature can have impinged on that depressed mind, it is useless to try to investigate. This much, however, we may say: that those events must have existed. If they had not, the expression of that dispiritedness would have been, not the verbal and psychological content of the tragedies, but nothing at all. Depression leads to inaction; the writing of plays is, however, action. It may have been born of three things: (1) the need to write them—the practical need, we mean; (2) the recuperative power of a temperament not organically (only) depressed, reacting in the intervals of depression against depression itself; (3) the stress of extreme suffering—not depression, but suffering—acting like a lash on a cowering sadness, driving it into expression as into a lair, into objectivity as into an outlet from self, for, as Goethe said, "Action consoles of all."

The presence of all three factors can be predicted. The need to write these plays shows in the intensity and bitterness of the phrases that voice depression—not quiet, half-peaceful, and somewhat indifferent, as in *The Tempest*, but restless, somber, dully forceful. Nothing depresses more than the necessity to act when there is no desire to act. The recuperative power of the temperament, the great boon of Shakespeare's hysteria, shows in the fact that there is no lowering, but a heightening, of his genius. The part of that due to natural growth need not and cannot be denied. But the overcuriousness of expression, the overintelligence that some-times even dulls the edge of dramatic intuition (as in Laertes' phrases before mad Ophelia) cannot be explained on that line, because these are not peculiarities [in the] growth of genius but [are] more natural to its youth than to its virile age. They are patently the effort of the intellect to crush out emotion, to cover depression, to oust preoccupation of distress by preoccupation of thought. But the lash of outward mischance (no one can now say what, or how brought about, and to what degree by the man himself) is very evident in the constant choice of abnormal mental states for the basis of these tragedies. Only the dramatic mind wincing under the strain of outer evil thus projects itself instinctively into figures which must utter wholly the derangement that is partly its own.

✖ The Manipulations of Sensibility

1. The Levels of Lyric Poetry

The first level of lyric poetry is that in which the poet, of an intensely emotive temperament, expresses spontaneously or reflectively that temperament and those emotions. It is the most common type of lyric poet; also, it is the least estimable, as a type. The intensity of emotion proceeds, in general, from the unity of temperament, so this type of lyric poet is generally monotonic, and his poems revolve about a fixed, usually small number of emotions. Therefore, it is a commonplace to say of this type of poet, as is understandably noted, that one is "a love poet," another "a nostalgic poet," a third "a melancholic poet."

The second level of lyric poetry is that in which the poet, being more intellectual or imaginative or even simply more cultured, no longer has the simplicity of emotions or their limitations that distinguish the poet on the first level. He will also be typically a lyric poet in the general sense of the term but will not be a monotonic poet.

The third level of lyric poet is that in which the poet, more intellectual still, begins to depersonalize, not just because he feels, but because he thinks he feels—feels states of the soul that he really does not possess, simply because he understands them. We are on the threshold of dramatic poetry in its innermost essence. The temperament of the poet, be that as it may, is dissolved by the intelligence. His work will be unified solely by style, that ultimate reduction of his spiritual unity, of his coexistence with himself. Thus there is Tennyson, writing both "Ulysses" and "The Lady of Shalott," and even more so, there is Browning, writing what he called "dramatic poems" that aren't dialogues but monologues revealing various souls, with whom the poet does not identify or pretend to, and frequently does not even want to.

The fourth level of lyric poetry, much rarer, is that in which the poet, more intellectual still but equally imaginative, fully undergoes depersonalization. He not only feels but lives the states of soul that he does not possess directly. In a great number of instances he will fall into dramatic poetry, properly speaking, as did Shakespeare, mainly a lyric poet raised to the dramatic through the surprising level of depersonalization he achieved. In one instance or another he will continue to be, however dramatically, a lyric poet. And it is the same for Browning (*ut supra*). Now, not even the style defines the unity of the man; only what is intellectual in the style denotes it. Thus in Shakespeare, in whom the unexpected prominence of phrase, the subtlety and complexity of expression, are the only things that make the speech of Hamlet approximate to that of King Lear, of Falstaff, of Lady Macbeth. And likewise the Browning seen through *Men and Women* and the *Dramatic Poems*.

Let us suppose, however, that the poet, always avoiding dramatic poetry, externally such, nevertheless advances one rung up the ladder of depersonalization. Certain states of soul, thought and not felt—but felt imaginatively and therefore experienced—will come to define for him a fictive person that he could sincerely feel. . . .

1930

2. Extensions of the Lyric Personality

Some figures I insert in stories or in the subtitles of books and give my name to what they say; others I project totally and do not give my name except to say that I made them. The types of figures are distinguished as follows: to those I totally detach, whose style is inappropriate to me and—if the figure demands it—even the opposite of my own. In the figures I subscribe to there's no difference from my own style except for a few inevitable details, without which they would be indistinguishable from one another.

I shall compare some of these figures so as to indicate by example in what such differences consist.

The assistant bookkeeper Bernardo Soares and the Baron de Teive—both figures are other me's—write in substantially the same manner, the same grammar, and same type and form of decorum; that is, they write in the same style, for better or worse, that I do. I compare the two because they are examples of the same phenomenon—unadaptability to the reality of life and, what's more, unadaptability for the same reasons and motives. However, while the Portuguese in Baron de Teive and in Bernardo Soares is the same, the style differs in that the nobleman's is intellectual, stripped of imagery, a bit—how shall I put it?—stiff and limited; and the style of the bourgeois is musically and pictorially fluid and rather architectonic. The nobleman thinks clearly, and controls his emotions, although not his feelings; the bookkeeper controls neither his emotions nor his feelings, and his thinking subserves his feelings.

There are notable similarities, on the other hand, between Bernardo Soares and Álvaro de Campos. But right from the start there surges in Álvaro de Campos a carelessness in the use of Portuguese, a looseness of images, in a style more intimate and less willful than that of Soares.

Accidents occur when I distinguish one from another that weigh on my inner understanding like great burdens—for example, in distinguishing some musical composition by Bernardo Soares from a composition of the same quality by me.

There are moments in which I compose impetuously, with a perfection I marvel at; and I marvel without immodesty because, not believing in any fragment of human liberty whatever, I marvel at what occurs in me in the same way I'd marvel at its occurring in others—in two strangers.

Only a great intuition may serve as a compass in the wasteland of the soul; only with a feeling that makes use of the intelligence without being assimilated by it, while still being established in this feeling through it, can these dream figures be distinguished in their reality from one another.

In such extensions of personality or, rather, inventions of different personalities, there are two levels or types to be revealed to the reader—if he follows them—by distinct characteristics. On the first level, the personality distinguishes itself by its own ideas and feelings, distinct from mine, so that on the lower level of this grade it is distinguished by ideas framed by ratiocination or argumention that are not mine—or if they are, I do not recognize them. *The Anarchist Banker* is an example of this lower level; the *Book of Disquietude* and the character of Bernardo Soares are the higher level.

The reader should note that although I am publishing—it publishes itself—the *Book of Disquietude* under the name of a certain Bernardo Soares, assistant bookkeeper in the city of Lisbon, I did not include it in the *Fictions of the Interlude*. This is because Bernardo Soares, distinct from me in ideas, feelings, modes of perception, and understanding, is not distinct from me in expository style. I represent a different character by means of the style that is natural to me, not having more than the inevitable distinction of special tone that the very speciality of emotions necessarily projects.

In the authors of the *Fictions of the Interlude,* not only the ideas and feelings differ from mine: the very technique of composition, the very style, is different from mine. Thus each character is created as integrally different and is not merely construed differently. That is why verse predominates in the *Fictions of the Interlude.* It is more difficult to make oneself into another in prose.

Aristotle divided poetry into lyric, elegiac, epic, and dramatic. Like all classifications that are well conceived, it is useful and clear; like all classifications, it is false. Literary genres are not so easily separated, and if we look closely at what they involve, we see that there's a continual gradation from lyric to dramatic poetry. In effect, and going back to the origins of dramatic poetry (Aeschylus, for example), it is more accurate to say we find lyric poetry placed in the mouths of various characters.

On the first level of lyric poetry, the poet, who is focused on his feeling, expresses that feeling. If, however, he is someone of many different and shifting feelings, his expression will take in a multiplicity of characters unified only by temperament and style. One step further up the poetic ladder and we have the poet of varied and fictive feelings, given more to the imaginative than to sentiment and living each mood intellectually rather than emotionally. Such a poet will express himself through a multiplicity of characters not united by temperament and style, because imagination displaces temperament and intelligence displaces feeling, with style as the only unifying element. Another step up the same ladder of depersonalization, or let us say of the imagination, and we have the poet who, during each of his various moods, gives himself over to that mood so completely that he is entirely depersonalized; who, analytically experiencing that state of mind, makes of it the expression of another character, and in this way the style itself tends to vary. Take the final step and you have a poet who is various poets, a dramatic poet writing lyric poetry. Each mood cluster, similar to each other, will become a character, with its own style and with feelings that perhaps differ from, even contradict, the feelings of the poet in his living person. And he will have raised lyric poetry—or whatever literary form is substantially analogous to lyric poetry—into dramatic poetry, without, however, giving it dramatic form, either explicitly or implicitly.

Let us suppose that a supreme depersonalizer like Shakespeare, instead of creating the character Hamlet as part of a play, created it as a simple person with no play. He would have written a drama, so to speak, of a single person, an extended, analytical monologue. It would not be valid to go looking for a definition of the feelings and thoughts of Shakespeare in such a character unless the character was a failure, because it's the poor dramaturge who reveals himself.

For whatever motive of temperament, which I don't propose to go into—nor is it important that I do—I constructed inside myself various characters different from one another and from myself, such characters to whom I attributed different poems that are not like those that I, with my feelings and ideas, would write.

This is how the poems of Caeiro, Ricardo Reis, and Álvaro de Campos are to be considered. One should not seek in any one of them ideas or sentiments that are mine, because many of them express ideas that I do not accept, sentiments I never had. They should simply be read as they are, which is, moreover, the way to read.

An example: I wrote with astonishment and repugnance the eighth poem of *The Keeper of Sheep*, with its infantile blasphemy and its absolute antireligiosity. In my own apparently real person, living socially and objectively, I neither use blasphemy nor am I antireligious. Alberto Caeiro, however, as I conceived him, *is* like that, so he has to write like that whether I wish it or not, whether I think like him or not. To deny myself the right to do this would be the same as denying Shakespeare the right to give expression to the soul of Lady Macbeth on the basis that he as poet was neither a woman nor, as far as we know, a hysteroepileptic, or to attribute to him a hallucinatory tendency and an ambition that does not flinch from committing a crime. If this holds for fictitious characters in a play, it also holds for fictitious characters outside of a play, since it is legitimate because they are fictitious and not because they are in a play.

It would seem unnecessary to explicate something so evident and intuitively grasped. It happens, however, that human stupidity is enormous and human benevolence not remarkable.

3. Notes on a Non-Aristotelian Aesthetic *by Álvaro de Campos (excerpt)*

I call the Aristotelian aesthetic that which assumes that the end of art is beauty or, better said, the establishment in others of the same impression as that which is born from the contemplation or sensation of beautiful things. . . .

I believe that I am able to formulate an aesthetic based not on the idea of beauty but rather on that of *force*—using the word *force,* of course, in its abstract scientific sense, because if it were based on the commonplace meaning, it would be a matter of a certain manner, merely a disguised form of beauty. This new aesthetic, while accepting as good a large number of classical works—accepting them, however, for other than Aristotelian reasons, which were naturally also those of the classical authors—creates the possibility of constructing new kinds of artworks that could not be foreseen or accepted by anyone who upholds the Aristotelian theory.

For me, art is, *like all activity,* a sign of force or energy; but as art is produced by human beings and is therefore a product of life, the forms of force revealed in art are the forms of force revealed in life. Now, vital force is twofold: integration and disintegration, anabolism and catabolism, as the physiologists call it. Without the coexistence and equilibrium of these two forces there is no life, because pure integration is absence of life and pure disintegration is death. Because these two forces essentially oppose as well as balance one another in order to maintain life, as long as there is life, life is an action automatically and intrinsically accompanied by its corresponding reaction. And it is in the automatic nature of the reaction that the specific phenomenon of life resides. . . .

The value of a life, that is, the vitality of an organism, resides in the intensity of its reactive force. . . . Now art, made out of feelings and in order to create feeling (without which it would be science or propaganda), is rooted in sensibility. Sensibility is therefore the *life* of art. Within sensibility, however, there is necessarily the action and reaction that make the art of living, the disintegration and integration that, creating an equilibrium, give life. If the force of integration were to penetrate art from outside of sensibility, it would come from *outside* of life; it would not be a matter of automatic or natural reaction but rather of a mechanical and artificial reaction. . . .

In contrast, therefore, to the Aristotelian aesthetic requiring that the individual generalize or humanize his sensibility, which is necessarily particular and personal, in this theory the desired course is the opposite: It is the general that should be particularized, the human that should be made personal, the "outside" that should be made "inside." . . .

All art begins with sensibility and is actually based on it. But whereas the Aristotelian artist subordinates sensibility to intelligence so as to make the sensibility human and universal (or, in other words, to make it accessible and pleasing, and thus capable of enthralling others), the non-Aristotelian artist subordinates everything to his own sensibility, converting everything into the substance of sensibility. In this way, his sensibility, made *abstract* as intelligence (without ceasing to be sensibility), made a *transmitter* out of will (without its thereby being will), becomes a *transmitting focal point, both abstract and sensitive,* that forces others, whether they wish it or not, to feel what he felt. It thus dominates them by inexplicable force, as the strongest athlete dominates the weakest, as the spontaneous dictator subjugates an entire people (because he is a complete synthesis and is therefore stronger than a condensation of himself), as the founder of a religion dogmatically and absurdly converts alien souls to the substance of a doctrine that at heart is nothing if not himself.

The true artist is a dynamogenic focal point; the false or Aristotelian artist is simply a transforming apparatus destined to do no more than convert the continuous current of his own sensibility into periodic currents of alien intelligence. . . .

My aesthetic theory is based on the idea of force, as opposed to the Aristotelian theory, which is based on the idea of beauty. Now, the idea of beauty can be a force. When the idea of beauty is an idea of the sensibility, an *emotion* and not an idea, a sensitive disposition of temperament, this idea of beauty is a force. It is not a force only when it is a simple *intellectual* idea of beauty.

Thus Greek art is great, even according to my criterion—*especially* according to my criterion. Beauty, harmony, proportion were not concepts of the intelligence for the Greeks but intimate tendencies of their sensibility. That is why they were an *aesthetic people* seeking and demanding beauty, *all of them, in everything* and *always.* That is why they *emanated* so demonstrably their sensitivity over the future world, to which we still live subjected, because of their tyranny over us. But our sensibility is already so different— worked over as it has been by so many and such complex social forces—that we can no longer receive this emanation through sensibility but only through the intelligence. . . .

Finally, up until now, when for the first time an authentic doctrine of non-Aristotelian art appears, there have been only three manifestations of it. The first is in the astonishing poems of Walt Whitman; the second is in the more than astonishing poems of my master Caeiro; the third is in the two odes ("Triumphal Ode" and "Maritime Ode") that I published in *Orpheu*. I do not ask whether this is immodesty. I affirm that it is true.

4. Ultimatum (excerpt)

ATTENTION

I Proclaim First of All
The Law of Malthusian Sensibility

The stimulants of sensibility increase in geometrical progression; sensibility itself merely increases in arithmetical progression.

. . . Sensibility, taken here in its broadest sense, is the origin of all civilized creation. But only when such sensibility is adapted to the milieu in which it functions does total creation occur; the greatness and force of the resultant work is commensurate with the degree of interaction between the creating sensibility and its environment. . . .

Hence, there must be at certain periods of civilization a failure of sensibility to adjust to the milieu that stimulates it—a breakdown, in other words. This is what's happening in our epoch, with its incapacity to create great values as a result of this maladjustment. . . .

Because what is natural and instinctive has failed, we are faced with a dilemma: the death of civilization or artificial adjustment. To avoid the death of civilization, I proclaim, secondly, THE NECESSITY OF ARTIFICIAL ADJUSTMENT.

What is artificial adjustment?

It is an act of sociological surgery. It is the violent transformation of the sensibility to make its response parallel, at least for a time, to the growth of its stimulants. . . .

What must be eliminated from the contemporary psyche?

Obviously the most recent *stable acquisition* of the spirit—that is, the general acquisition of the civilized human spirit that immediately preceded the establishment of our contemporary civilization. . . .

What is the most recent acquisition of the general human spirit?

It must be Christian dogmas, because the Middle Ages, dynamic epoch of systematic Christianity, precedes immediately and forever the flowering of our civilization, and the Christian principles are contradicted by the sound teachings of modern science.

Artificial adjustment will spontaneously result only when spiritual acquisitions permeated by Christianity are eliminated.

I THEREFORE PROCLAIM, THIRDLY, THE ANTI-CHRISTIAN SURGICAL INTERVENTION.

This can come about, as is evident, by the elimination of the three notions, dogmas, or attitudes that Christianity allowed to penetrate the very substance of the human psyche.

Concrete explanation:

1. ABOLITION OF THE DOGMA OF PERSONALITY. . . .

2. ABOLITION OF THE CONCEPT OF INDIVIDUALISM. . . .

3. ABOLITION OF THE DOGMA OF PERSONAL OBJECTIVITY. . . .

But what Method, what type of collective operation, can organize these results among the men of the future? . . .

If I knew the Method, I would myself be that entire generation!

But I see only the Way; I don't know where it will lead.

In any case, I proclaim as necessary the coming of the Humanity of the Engineers! . . .

I proclaim the arrival of a mathematical humanity, a perfect humanity! . . .

And I also proclaim that: First,

THE SUPERMAN WILL BE NOT THE STRONGEST BUT THE MOST COMPLETE!

And I also proclaim: Secondly,

THE SUPERMAN WILL BE NOT THE TOUGHEST BUT THE MOST COMPLEX!

And I also proclaim: Thirdly,

THE SUPERMAN WILL BE NOT THE MOST FREE BUT THE MOST HARMONIOUS!

I proclaim this aloud from the rooftops, at the entrance of the Tagus, with my back to Europe, arms raised, staring fixedly at the Atlantic, and abstractly greeting the Infinite!

5. Letter to Marinetti

My dear Marinetti:

I have not written you earlier because politics, which I have now almost altogether set aside, and also lust have left me almost no time to fulfill other duties and enjoy other pleasures. But, at any rate, here I am.

I was already acquainted with some of the manifestoes which you have sent me, and for which I thank you very much. Besides these, I had also read Boccioni's fine book on futurist painting and sculpture. I am therefore not altogether ignorant in the manner of futurism; I am even to a certain extent on your side.

I think, however, that futurism ought to develop very much and to abandon its extreme exclusivism. It seems to me that your idea of history is too little futurist, and that you figure to yourselves a far too regular historic development. In evolution we do not find a regularly ascending line; on the contrary, development takes place in a violent and cataclysmic manner, in which gains are achieved only through fundamental losses. And all this occurs in a very labyrinthic manner which produces vertigo: Here you have real futurism in history. Social values are scattered almost haphazard over times and places, and what there is of progress appears only through the loss of something which must be produced anew that the Infinite may at last be established. In the Infinite, which is the supreme futurist aspiration, all values should be realized without the possibility of the loss of any of them. If there be losses in evolution, even through manifest gains, let those losses be but momentary. In no other way can the Infinite emerge, since nothing must be lacking to it.

Modern civilization, which conceived futurism before the war, possesses new elements that were hitherto unknown. But, on the other hand, it no longer possesses elements, social values, that are as important as its own [. . . once were.] Something has been gained, but through several losses. Modern civilization has acquired new aspects of Existence, but it has lost other aspects. It is therefore necessary that the Future should be the supreme synthesis of all that has been lost and of all that exists still, so that it may engender the Infinite, to which nothing is ever lacking, from which no single aspect of Existence is absent. It is this definitive state of Life that must be prepared, so that we may infinitize ourselves for ever.

The Infinite, since it is continuous, is a multiplicity-one, and therefore the civilization that can be identified with it must not be divided into several peoples, for it must be but one people, the perfect synthesis of all the peoples of the Universe. In this synthesis, nothing must be missing; then all the scattered aspects of Existence, which are the divers peoples and individuals, small worlds of universal impressions, will rule together in the Infinite, which will mingle them with each other, without the sacrifice of any of them. In this way, each individual and each people should develop itself as much as possible, and yet their purpose should not be individual or nationalistic, since it must rather act so that nothing may be lost before the establishment of the synthesis-Infinity, to which nothing is lacking. If a people were to be sacrificed, that would mean that a multitudinary aspect of Existence would be lost for ever; and for this reason I seek nationalism with a purely ultranationalist purpose: synthesis is a [whole, in] which nothing is lacking. Now it is not only in space that we must take into consideration the different peoples and civilizations, the several scattered aspects of infinite

Existence; we must consider them also through all times, throughout all lost history. Many things have disappeared, and they must emerge again, rejuvenated and infinitized: In each element of the Infinite all the other elements are included and this, because the Infinite is continuous, is pure Unity all through the fact of being Multiplicity.

If modern civilization has a spirit of Inexpression, of essential Void (Vacuum), which is the basis (essence) of your "music hall sensibility," the Middle Ages, for instance, knew how to live splendidly the spirit of the Supernatural, which must be made to reappear. Yet in the Middle Ages this spirit is imperfect, because it is not excessive, as it will be when it is combined with the spirit of Void (Vacuum), which is the essence of our civilization. Infinity-Void, God-Void: This is what must be sought. Through this supernatural, astral Void, the forms, the phantoms of Existence, altogether real and altogether false and in an altogether labyrinthic manner, glide essentially in Vertigo with each other. Each presupposes all the others and creates them in itself and qua itself, by the excess of its nature, as I shortly make evident; and then each exists but labyrinthically by the others and for the others, that is to say, they all exist only relatively some to the others. The Relative is not the simple Nothingness, and yet it has the spirit of Nothingness all the while it expresses (throughout the fact of its expressing) a creative act, an altogether anim[ist]ic act (an act of pure existence), that which manifests itself (shows itself) in things in their conceiving, in their creating other things, which therefore exist only by them and for them, in fine, only relatively to them. In this way, Life, which is a relativist phantomogeny where there is but Indecision, where there is but Vertigo, impregnates itself with Void as well as with Absolute, which is pure Existence, pure creative animism, as I shall shortly make quite evident.

This Astral Void, this altogether anim[ist]ic Void-Infinity, this Void-Phantom in Vertigo (in labyrinthizing-Vertigo) is as awful as it is sublime, being the pure Essence of Life. It expresses the absolute creative power (it is the absolutely, infinitely creative act expressed in pure relativity); it is the pure, the divine Anim[ist]ic-Creating, so pure that there is no question of an animism creator of

77

a being, but of an animism in itself, purely in abstract. It is because there is no longer being in this animism that we have a pure void in this pure act of anim[ist]ic existence; and it is this that sublimates awfully the essence of Life, that essence, as sublime as it is awful, of infinite Void-Phantom in Vertigo.

If we have here a creative power, we have here doubtlessly the spirit of God, the Holy Spirit (Ghost) of Death which is the essence of the whole World! And I refer to Death because we naturally conceive [of] Death as an altogether abstract life, full of spiritual darkness, and of an altogether animized infinite void: Animism and void are indeed the things proper to death.

It is therefore a new Religion and a new Church that I wish to announce, and both one and the other have a distinctly futuristic character. The rule of the Void in a pure spirit of Relative-Creating, the Indecision-Vertigo of all, the pure gliding of forms-phantoms which are lost each in another in an altogether labyrinthic manner, in a manner distinctly vertigic, all this is markedly futuristic. And it is a glory for Futurism that Religion itself can profit by its doctrines.

The Paracletian Church, whose foundation God commands me to announce, is an essentially Futuristic Church! Let us then raise the bloody flag of Revolt against the rotten carcass of the Vatican!

Like you, I condemn simple rationalism; yet my opinion is that we must go beyond it. Now to go beyond it, and thus to attain the Infinite, we must traverse it first. The simple intuition, or rather the simple immediate impression of things, is not enough. We must know, understand, feel altogether purely the intimate (inner) reason of things, and how they are engendered (produced). It is true that Futurism seeks in relativity, that is, in what it calls physical transcendentalism, the creative reason of impressions, but it seeks only their physical, outer, superficial and empirical reason, and not their metaphysical, intimate, deep abysmic one! It is only the senses that seek that one, while the metaphysical reason of things is found (out) by pure thought in an altogether emotional purity. I can foresee your objection: "But it is thought itself that we absolutely condemn." I am not of that opinion; I wish only that thought may transcend itself and attain the supreme state of Vertigo! You are on this side of thought (on the near side of thought); I prefer its pure other side.

1917

6. The Anarchist Banker: A Fiction

We had just finished dinner. My friend the banker, big businessman, and well-known monopolist sat in front of me, smoking without a thought in the world. The conversation, which had been lapsing, died down. I tried to rekindle it between us by resorting to the first idea that popped into my head. I turned toward him, smiling.

"It's true: I was told the other day that you were once an anarchist. . . ."

"Were, no: Have been and still am. I haven't changed in that respect. *I am* an anarchist."

"That's quite wonderful! You, an anarchist! In what way are you an anarchist? . . . Only if you give the word some meaning different from . . ."

"Different from the usual? No, not at all. I use the word in its usual sense."

"Do you mean to say that you're an anarchist in just the same way as those chaps in the worker's union are? So there's no difference at all between you and those fellows with the bomb and in the unions?"

"Difference, difference, there is one. . . . Obviously there's a difference. But it's not what you think. Do you doubt my social ideas are the same as theirs?"

"Oh, I see now! You're an anarchist in theory; but in practice . . ."

"I'm as much an anarchist in practice as I am in theory. And as for practice, I'm more so—I'm much more of an anarchist than those chaps you mention. My whole life proves it."

"What?"

"My whole life proves it, dear boy. It's you who've never given such matters a close look. That's why it seems to you I'm talking nonsense or I'm joking with you."

"Well, man, I don't understand it one bit! ... Unless ... unless you've given up on life and become antisocial, and in that sense anarchism ... "

"I've already told you that's not so; I mean I already said I'm not using the word anarchism in any sense different from the usual."

"Quite right. ... I still don't understand. ... Do you wish to tell me, sir, that there's no difference between your truly anarchist theories and the way you live—your way of life now? You want me to believe that you live exactly in the same way those chaps commonly called anarchists do?"

"No, no, that's not it. What I mean is, there's no divergence whatever between my theories and the way I live; there's absolute accord. As for not living my life like those syndicalist fellows with the bombs—that's true. But it's their own life that's lived apart from anarchism, apart from their ideals. Not mine. In me—yes, in me, banker, financier, monopolist, if you will—in me anarchist theory and practice are exactly fused. You compared me with those fool syndicalists with the bombs to indicate that I'm different from them. I am, but here's the difference: They (yes, they, and not I) are anarchists in theory only; I am an anarchist in theory and in practice both. They are anarchists and stupid fools; I am an anarchist and enlightened. Which is to say, old boy, it's I who am the true anarchist. They—the syndicalists with the bombs (I'd been there too but dropped all that precisely because my anarchism is authentic)—they are the dregs of anarchism, they are the prostitutes of the great libertarian doctrine."

"The devil wouldn't believe his ears! This is astonishing! But how do you reconcile your life—I mean, your life as a banker and businessman—with anarchist theories? How do you account for it, if you say that you understand anarchist theories in exactly the usual way everyone else understands them? And are you, although you're on top, telling me you're different from them by being *more* of an anarchist than they are—is that it?"

"Exactly."

"I don't understand a word."

"But you seriously want to?"

80

"Absolutely everything."

He took the dead cigar out of his mouth and slowly relit it; he made sure the match went out and placed it on the edge of the ashtray. Then, raising his momentarily lowered head, he said:

"Listen. I was born in poverty, a member of the working class in the city. I inherited nothing good, as you can imagine, either in social condition or in future prospects, except that I possessed, as I'm told, a naturally lucid intelligence and a more or less strong will. But those were natural gifts, which would not improve my low birth.

"I was a common laborer; I worked and life was hard. In a word, I was one of the masses and shared their lot. I don't say I actually starved to death, but I came close to it. But as for that matter, let it pass; it wouldn't have changed anything that happened or that I am about to tell you, either of what my life was like then or of what it's like now.

"In brief, I was a common laborer. Like all the rest, I worked because I had to work, and I worked as little as possible. What I was, was intelligent. Whenever I could, I'd read things, discuss things, and so, since I wasn't stupid, there grew inside me a great dissatisfaction and a great disaffection with my fate and the social conditions that had made it so. I've already told you, in all honesty, that my fate could have been worse than it was, but at that time it seemed to me I was a creature on whom fate had worked all its injustices at once, and that social conventions had disabled me. And that's where things stood when I was twenty years old—twenty-one at most—the time I became an anarchist."

He paused a moment, turned somewhat closer to me, and bending his head forward, spoke:

"I was always more or less lucid. I felt rebellious. I wanted to understand my rebelliousness. I became a conscientious and convinced anarchist—as conscientious and convinced as I am today."

"And the theory you hold today is the same one you held back then?"

"The same. Anarchist theory—the authentic theory—is just one thing. I hold it now as I always have since becoming an anarchist. As you'll soon see. . . . I was telling you that being lucid by nature, I became a conscientious anarchist. Well, what is an anarchist? He's a rebel against the injustice of being born *socially* unequal—basically, that's all he is. And from that there follows, as you'll see, the rebellion against social conventions that made such inequality possible. What I'm now trying to indicate to you is the psychological impetus, so to speak, that turns people to anarchism; we'll address the theoretical aspects of the subject later. For the moment, you'll surely understand what rebellion would be like for an intelligent chap in my circumstances. What has he seen of the world? Born the son of a millionaire, protected at the start from such misfortunes—and they're not just a few—that wealth can obviate or at least attenuate; another, born in wretched circumstances, being, as a child, one more mouth to feed in a family with too many mouths for the food available. Someone who's born a count or a marquis, and for that reason has everyone's esteem, does things accordingly; someone else, born as I was, has to tread softly in order to be treated at least like a human being. Those who are born with the wherewithal for studying, traveling, gaining experience, grow more 'intelligent,' as they say, than those having the natural gift of intelligence. And that's the way it always is everywhere. . . .

"So much for the injustices of nature; we can't get rid of them. But as for the injustices of society and its conventions, why shouldn't we get rid of them? I grant—I don't even have the choice—that a man should be superior to me by natural endowment: talent, strength, energy. I do not grant that he should be my superior for qualities accrued later, which he did not possess on leaving his mother's womb, but which were put at his disposal by chance as soon as he appeared on earth: wealth, social position, a life of ease, and so on. So my anarchism was born from the rebelliousness I've been trying to describe to you—an anarchism, as I've already told you, which I still subscribe to today with no change whatever."

Again he paused momentarily as if to consider how to proceed. He inhaled a mouthful of cigar smoke and expelled it slowly from the chair he sat in opposite me. He turned and was about to start again. But I interrupted him.

"One question, out of simple curiosity: Why is it you chose anarchism particularly? You could have chosen socialism or some other extremist cause that wasn't so remote. That would all have answered for your rebelliousness. . . . I suspect from what you say that you mean by anarchism (and I find it a very good definition) the revolt against conventions and social formulas and the urge and power to abolish them all. . . .

"That's it exactly."

"Why did you take this extreme recourse and not something else more moderate . . . ?

"I'll tell you. I considered it all. It's clear I picked up various theories in the tracts I was reading. I chose the anarchist doctrine—as you quite rightly say—for reasons I'll put to you in two words."

For a moment he looked off into empty space. Then he turned to me.

"The true evil, the only evil, are the conventions and the social myths superimposed on natural realities—everything from family to money, from religion to the state. People are born male or female—I mean, born to become adults, men or women; they are not born, according to good natural justice, to be a husband, or to be rich or poor, just as they are not born to be Catholic or Protestant or Portuguese or English. And all these things one becomes because of social myths. Now, why are these social myths evil? *Because they are myths, because they are not natural.* Money is just as evil as the state, the institution of the family as evil as religion. If instead of these myths there were others, they'd be just as bad *because they too would be myths,* because they too would be superimposed and would intervene in natural realities. Any system, except pure anarchism, that seeks to abolish all myths, each and every one of them entirely *is also a myth.* To employ all our desire, all our effort, all our intelligence in order to establish or contribute to the establishment of one social myth in place of another is an absurdity, if not a crime, *because it is done to cause a social disturbance with the express aim of leaving everything unchanged.* If we find social myths unjust because

83

they crush or oppress what is natural in man, why employ our energy to supplant them with other myths if we can use it to destroy them all?

"This seems to me to be conclusive. But suppose it were not; let's suppose someone objects that, true as this may be, the anarchist system cannot be made practicable. So let's look into that side of the question.

"Why should the anarchist system not be practicable? We of the avant-garde start from the principle that not only is the present system unjust but, because there is justice, there's the advantage in changing the system for another that's more just. If we don't think in this way, then we don't have avant-garde ideas; we're bourgeois. Now where does this criterion of *justice* come from? From the fact that it's *natural and true,* as opposed to social myths and the lies of convention. So what's natural is what's totally natural, not half or a quarter or an eighth natural. Very well. Now, of the two things, one: Either what's natural is socially practicable or it's not; in other words, either society can be natural or society is essentially mythical and cannot be natural in any form whatever. If society can be natural, then the anarchist or free society ought to be possible and should be, because it's an entirely natural society. If society cannot be natural, if (for whatever reason, it doesn't matter) it must perforce be mythical, we should choose the lesser evil: Let's make it the most natural society possible so that it may become the most just possible. What's the most natural possible myth? None is natural in itself, because it's mythical: The most natural in our case would be that which *seems* most natural, which *feels* most natural. What is it that seems most natural or that feels most natural? It's what we are most used to. (You understand: What's natural is what's instinctive; and that which, not being instinctive, seems totally instinctive, is habit.) Smoking isn't natural, it's not an instinctive need, but if we are in the habit of smoking it becomes natural for us, comes to be felt like an instinctive need. Now what is the social myth that constitutes a habit for us? It's the present system, the bourgeois system. So we must, quite logically, either believe the natural society possible and be defenders of anarchism, or we must believe it impossible and be defenders of the bourgeois regime. There's no intermediate hypothesis. You see that?"

"Yes, it's conclusive."

"Not entirely, just yet. . . . There's still another objection of the same sort to get rid of. . . . One can agree that the anarchist system is practicable but may doubt that it's practicable *overnight*—in other words, that one can pass from a bourgeois to a free society without going through one or more intermediate states or regimes. Whoever raises such an objection considers anarchist society good and practicable but has the impression that there must be some sort of transition between it and bourgeois society.

"Very well, then. Let's suppose that this is so. What would that intermediate state be? Our goal is a free or anarchist society; that intermediate state, however, can only be a preparatory state for humanity preceding a free society.

"Such preparation is either material or simply mental, meaning it's either a series of material or social realizations that permit humanity to adapt itself to the free society, or it's simple propaganda, growing gradually in influence, that begins to prepare society mentally to desire and accept it.

"Let's take the first instance, the gradual and material adaptation of humanity to a free society. It's impossible; it's more than impossible—it's absurd. There's no material adaptation to anything that doesn't already exist. None of us can adapt himself materially to the social milieu of the twenty-third century without knowing what is will be like; and one can't adapt materially because the twenty-third century and its social setup do not materially exist. We therefore conclude that, in passing from bourgeois society to free society, the only aspect available for adaptation, evolution, or transition is the mental aspect, *and the gradual adaptation of the spirit to the idea of a free society.* . . . At any rate, with respect to material adaptation, there's still another hypothesis . . . "

"Damn all those hypotheses! . . . "

"The lucid man, old chap, is obliged to examine all possible objections and to refute them before he can be said to be certain of his doctrine. And, moreover, all this is in answer to a question you asked me. . . . "

"That's fine."

"As I said, with regard to material adaptation, there is, in any case, one other hypothesis. That concerns the revolutionary dictatorship."

"What about the revolutionary dictatorship?"

"As I explained it to you, there's no material adaptation to anything that doesn't yet exist materially. But if, by means of a sudden *coup*, the social revolution occurred, it would establish itself not as the free society (as humanity would not be ready for it) but as the dictatorship of those wanting to establish the free society. But there already exists—although still in embryo or just beginning—there already *materially* exists some sort of free society. Consequently there already exists something material to which society may adapt itself. And this is the argument that the cretins who defend 'the dictatorship of the proletariat' would use if they were capable of arguing or thinking. The argument clearly isn't theirs; it's mine. I offer it to myself as an objection, and, as I'm about to show you, it's false.

"A revolutionary regime (while it lasts, and whatever the goal it proposes or the idea that inspires it) is *materially* one thing only—a revolutionary regime. For a revolutionary regime means an armed dictatorship or, to put it more precisely, a despotic military regime, because an armed state is imposed on society by one part of it—the part that assumed power by way of revolution. What ensues? It follows that whatever gets adapted to such a regime, which is materially, immediately, nothing but a despotic military regime, is adapted in effect to a despotic military regime. The idea that guided the revolutionaries, or the end they had in view, vanishes completely in the social *reality*, which is occupied completely with the war-making phenomenon. So that what ensues from a revolutionary dictatorship—and will continue more and more to ensue from it—is a combative society of the dictatorial type, that is, military despotism. Nor can it ever be anything else. And it's always been so. I don't know much about history, but this I do know for certain—nor can I ever cease being certain about it. What occurred after the political agitations in Rome? The Roman Empire and its military despotism. What happened after the French Revolution? Napoleon

86

and his military despotism. And you'll see what's to come after the Russian revolution: something that will set back the achievement of a free society for decades and decades. Besides, what could you expect from a nation of illiterates and mystics?

"Anyway, that goes beyond the scope of our conv—You do understand my drift?"

"I understood it perfectly."

"Then you'll understand that I reached this conclusion: the aim: anarchist society, free society; the means: the passage, *without transition*, from bourgeois to free society. Such a passage would be made possible through an intense, complete, all-engulfing propaganda, so as to predispose all spirits and weaken all resistance. It's clear that by 'propaganda' I don't mean simply the spoken and written word, I mean everything: direct and indirect action, whatever can promote the free society and weaken any opposition to its advent. Thus, having scarcely any resistance to overcome, the social revolution, when it arrives, will be swift and easy and will not have to set up a revolutionary dictatorship, having nobody against whom to apply it. If it cannot be brought about in this way, then it's because anarchism is not realizable; and if anarchism is not realizable, then only bourgeois society is defensible and just, as I've shown.

"So there you have why and how I became an anarchist, and why and how I rejected as false and unnatural the other less daring social doctrines. And so, quickly now, let's get on with my story."

He struck a match and slowly lit his cigar. He concentrated on it, and after a while, continued:

"There were other fellows with ideas like mine. Mostly they were workers, but one and another weren't; all of us were poor and, as I recall, none of us exactly stupid. We had a certain urge to instruct ourselves, to know things, and, at the same time, the will to propagandize, to spread our ideas. We wanted for ourselves, and for others—for all of humanity—a new society, free from all those preconceptions that make men artificially unequal and that impose on them inferiorities, sufferings, strictures that Nature had not imposed. As for myself, what I read confirmed me in such opinions.

87

Of the cheap libertarian books available to me at the time—and there were a considerable lot—I read almost all. I went to the lectures and propaganda rallies of the period. Every book and every speech filled me with more certainty and justified my ideas. What I thought then—I repeat it to you, my friend—is what I think today; the only difference is that then I only thought it, and today I think it and practice it."

"Yes, to be sure; this is all very well, as far as you've gone. It's all quite feasible that you should have become an anarchist in such a way, and I see perfectly that you were an anarchist. There's no further need for you to prove it. What I'd like to know is how you turned into a banker . . . how you got to be one without contradiction. . . . That is, I can more or less guess. . . . "

"No, don't guess anything. . . . I know what you mean to say. . . . You're basing it all on the argument you've just finished listening to from me, and you conclude that I found anarchism impracticable, and therefore, as I told you, that bourgeois society alone is defensible and just. Isn't that so?

"Yes, I guessed something of the sort, more or less. . . . "

"But how could that be so when from the start of our conversation I told you repeatedly that I am an anarchist, not only that I was but continue to be one? If I had turned into a banker and businessman for the reason you suppose, I would not be an anarchist, I'd be a bourgeois."

"Yes, you're right. . . . But then, how the devil . . . ? Well, go on telling it to me. . . . "

"As I said, I was—always was—more or less lucid, and also a man of action; those were natural qualities—they weren't tucked into the cradle for me (assuming I had a cradle); I am what I brought out of it. All right, then. As an anarchist, I found being a passive one intolerable, just going about and listening to speeches and talking about it with friends. No: I had to do something about it! It was necessary to work and fight for the cause of the oppressed and the victims of social conventions! I decided to dedicate myself to the task, as much as I could. I began to think how I might be useful in the libertarian cause. I began to set up my plan of action.

88

"What is it an anarchist wants? Liberty—liberty for himself and for others, for all humanity. He wants to be free from the influence or pressure of the social myths; he wants to be free, from the time he's born and appears in the world, as he justly ought to be; and he wants such freedom for himself and for everybody else. Not everyone can be equal by Nature; some are born tall, others not; some strong, others weak; some more intelligent, others less so. But aside from that, all can be equal; only social myths prevent it. Those social myths have to be destroyed.

"It was necessary to destroy them. ... But one thing did not escape me: They had to be destroyed *for the sake of liberty,* without losing sight of the creation of a free society. Because one can just as well destroy existing social myths in order to create liberty, or prepare for its coming, as put in their place other social myths that are just as bad, because they are fictions. That's where one had to be careful. It was necessary to make sure of a plan of action, violent or not (because in fighting social injustices everything was legitimate), that would allow one to join in the destruction of social myths without, at the same time, hindering the creation of future liberty and, in creating it, not impede if possible, any part of that liberty.

"It's clear that such liberty, which one had to be careful not to disturb, was *future liberty* and, at present, *the liberty of the oppressed against social myths.* It's clear that we shouldn't mind disturbing the 'liberty' of the powerful, of the well-situated, of all those representing social myths and profiting from them. That's not liberty; it's the liberty to tyrannize, which is the opposite of liberty. On the contrary, it is what we had to think of blocking and fighting against. This all seems to be quite clear. ... "

"It's very, very clear. Do continue. ... "

"For whom does the anarchist want freedom? For all of humanity. In what way does one achieve liberty for all of humanity? By destroying completely all social myths. How can one completely destroy all social myths? I already anticipated and explained this to you when, to answer your question, I discussed the other avant-garde systems and described how and why I became an anarchist. ... You recall my conclusion?"

"I do."

"A sudden social revolution, sudden and crushing, to put an end at once to the society of the bourgeois regime in favor of the free society. This social revolution, prepared through an intense, continual labor of direct and indirect action, tending to unite morale for the advent of free society and to reduce into a comatose state all bourgeois resistance. Excuse my not repeating the reasons that lead inevitably to this conclusion from the anarchist point of view; I've already expounded them to you and you've taken them in."

"Yes."

"Such a revolution would preferably be worldwide, simultaneous at all points of the world, or at least at the important points; or, if not, spreading quickly from one point to another, but at all events, at each point—that is, with each nation—complete and devastating.

"Very well. What could *I* contribute toward such a goal? By myself alone I could do nothing for the world revolution, nor do anything for the world revolution in part, even in the country where I lived. What I could do, with everything in my power, was to lay the ground for such a revolution. I already told you how: by fighting, via all the available means, against the social myths; by never hindering, while engaged in fighting, either the propaganda for a free society or future freedom, or the present liberty of the workers, and still creating, if possible, something of the future freedom."

He let out a puff of smoke, paused briefly, began again.

"So here, my friend, is where I put my lucidity into action. It's all well and good to work for the future, I thought, to work for others to be free, certainly. But then, what about me? Am I nobody? If I were Christian I'd work gladly for the future of others, for then I'd have my reward in heaven; but, also if I were Christian, I wouldn't be an anarchist, because then such inequalities wouldn't be important in our short life: They'd only be conditions for our tribulations, and those would be rewarded in life eternal. But as I was no Christian, nor am I one now, I asked myself, for whom am I going to sacrifice everything for this? Furthermore, *why* am I going to sacrifice myself?

90

"I experienced moments of disbelief, and you understand that I was justified. . . . I'm a materialist, I thought; I've no other life but this one; why should I have to worry myself over social propaganda and inequalities and other cock-and-bull stories when I can enjoy and entertain myself much more if I don't concern myself with all that stuff. Whoever has only this life, whoever does not believe in life eternal, whoever doesn't admit to any law other than Nature, whoever opposes the state because it's unnatural, marriage because it's unnatural, money because it's unnatural, all the social myths because those are unnatural, why take on the burden of defending altruism and sacrifice for others or for humanity, if the altruism and the sacrifice are also unnatural? Yes, according to the same logic that I had demonstrated to myself that a man is not born to be a husband or to be Portuguese or to be rich or poor, I also demonstrated to myself that he isn't born to be a sharer, that he's not born except to be himself, however contrary this is to altruist and sharer and however exclusively egotistical.

"I debated the question with myself. Observe, I told myself, that we're born belonging to the human race and have the duty of sharing with all mankind. But was the idea of duty natural? Where did this idea of duty come from? If this idea of duty obliged me to sacrifice my well-being, my comfort, my instinct of preservation and other natural instincts, how does practicing this idea differ from practicing any social myth that produces in us the same effect?

"This idea of duty, of human solidarity, may only be considered natural *if it carries with it some egotistical reward,* because then, although it violates natural egotism, if it offers such egotism a reward, it is always, in the long run, unviolated. To sacrifice a pleasure simply to sacrifice it is unnatural; to sacrifice a pleasure for another's sake is still within the bounds of Nature: It is all right to choose one, if among two natural things both cannot be had at once. Now, what egotistic or natural reward can I gain by my dedication to the cause of a free society and future human happiness? Only the consciousness of having fulfilled a duty, of the effort toward a good end; and none of these things is a pleasure in itself but a pleasure, if it be one, derived from a myth, like that of being immensely rich, or the pleasure of having born into a good social condition.

"I must confess, dear friend, that I experienced moments of disbelief. ... I felt I was being disloyal to my principles and betraying them. ... But I soon overcame all of that. The idea of justice was right there, inside me, I thought. I felt it naturally. I felt that from such a preoccupation there was a higher duty to my own destiny. And I went ahead with my resolve."

"It doesn't seem to me that such a decision shows great lucidity on your part. ... You did not resolve the difficulty. ... You placed ahead of it an absolutely emotional impulse! ... "

"Undoubtedly. But what I am now telling you is the story of how I became an anarchist and how I continued to be one and still am. I want to set forth for you frankly the hesitations and the difficulties I had and how I conquered them. I agree that at that moment I overcame a logical difficulty emotionally and not rationally. But you'll see that later, when I arrived at a full understanding of anarchist doctrine, this difficulty, logically unanswered until then, had its complete and absolute solution."

"It's curious ... "

"It is. ... Now let me go on with my story. I had this difficulty and resolved it, for better or worse, as I told you. Then following that, along the same line of thinking, another difficulty arose that also troubled me a good deal.

"It was all right, let's say, that I should be disposed to sacrifice myself without any personal reward, that is, without any truly natural reward. But let's suppose that a future society doesn't care a whit about what I hope for, that there'd never be a free society; what the devil would I be sacrificing myself for in that case? To sacrifice myself for an idea without any personal reward, without gaining anything for my efforts on behalf of that idea—all right; but to sacrifice myself without at least having the certainty that what I labored for would one day exist, *without the idea itself having been won despite all my efforts*—that was a bit much. ... I just told you that I resolved this difficulty in the same emotional way that I had resolved the other; but I also warned you that this one resolved itself, like the other, automatically, by logic, once I reached full awareness of what my anarchism was. ... You'll see ... During the time about which I've.been telling you, I got out of my predicament with one or two empty phrases: 'I did my duty for the future; let the future do its duty for me. . . . ' Those or words to that effect. . . .

"I explained this conclusion, or, rather, these conclusions to my comrades and they agreed with me; they all agreed it was necessary to go straight ahead and act entirely for a free society. It's true that one or another of the more intelligent were a bit shocked by my argument, not because they didn't agree but because they'd never seen things so clearly or seen the sharp points that were involved in them. . . . But finally, they all agreed. . . . We'd all work for the great social revolution, for the free society, whether justified by the future or not! Among certain of us we formed a group and began a great propaganda campaign—great, of course, within the limits of what we could accomplish. For quite a while, in the midst of difficulties, confusions and harassments, we went on working for the anarchist ideal."

Having reached this point, the banker paused a while longer. He did not light his cigar, which had gone out again. Suddenly he smiled lightly and, with the air of one who reaches a crucial point in his story, fixed on me with greater intensity, clearing his voice and emphasizing his words.

"From that moment on," he said, "something new appeared. 'From that moment on' is a manner of speaking. I mean that after several months of propaganda, I began to notice in myself the existence of a new problem, and that was the most serious of them all—I mean it was crucial.

"You recall, don't you, how by a strict line of reasoning I defined what had to be the procedure for anarchist action? . . . A procedure or procedures by means of which one might contribute to the destruction of social myths without at the same time hindering the creation of future freedom, and furthermore without hindering in any way the slight present liberty, enjoyed by the oppressed, from social myths—a procedure that, if possible, would already create something of future liberty. . . .

"Well, then: Once this criterion was set down, I never failed to keep it in mind. However, from the time of embarking on our propaganda, of which I've been speaking, I discovered something. In our propaganda group—we weren't many: there were, give or take, around forty of us—the situation arose: *tyranny had come into being.*"

"Tyranny came into being? How so?"

"In the following way: ... There were those who were running the show and leading others around wherever they wanted to; there were those imposing on others and obliging them to be whatever they wished; some dragged others around by tricks and wiles wherever they wished. I'm not saying that they did this in important matters; actually, there weren't any important matters involved where they could do so. But the point is that this happened continually every day, not only in matters concerning propaganda, but also in the little things of daily life. Some imperceptibly became leaders, others imperceptibly became underlings. Some became bosses by main force, others by ruse. This was apparent in the smallest matters. For example: Two fellows were going down a street together; they came to the end of the block and one had to go to the right and the other to the left; each found it convenient to go his own way. But the one going to the left said to the other, 'Come on with me this way;' and the other replied—and it was true: 'Man, I can't; I've got to go that way'—for one reason or another. ... But in the end, against his own will and interest, he nevertheless went to the left with the other. ... This occurred once through persuasion, another time through simple insistence, a third time through some motive of a similar kind. ... It was never for any logical reason, and always in the domination and subordination there was something spontaneous as there was something instinctive. And so it went on this way, both in simple matters and in others, from the trivial to the most important. ... You understand the situation?"

"I do. But what the devil's so strange about it? All that sort of thing couldn't be more natural! ... "

"Well, maybe. We'll be getting to that. What I'm asking you to consider is that it's *exactly the opposite of anarchist doctrine*. Notice that this happened in a small group, a group neither influential nor important, a group entrusted with making no resolution of any serious problem or decision on any fundamental issue. Also note that this occurred among a group of people who came together particularly to do what they could to advance the anarchist cause—

that is, to oppose as much as possible the social myths and to create as much as possible future liberty. You've noted these two points closely?"

"I've noted them closely."

"Now note carefully what that portends. . . . A small group of sincere people (I promise you, they were sincere!) organized and brought together expressly to work for the cause of liberty, managed after several months to achieve only one positive and concrete thing: *the creation among them of a state of tyranny.* And notice the sort of tyranny. . . . It wasn't a tyranny stemming from active social myths, which, however regrettable, would be excusable, to an extent, though less so among us who were fighting those myths than among other people; but we were, in brief, living in the midst of a society based on such myths, and it wasn't wholly our fault if we couldn't flee from its active influence. But that's not what was at issue. Those who took command over the others, or who led them around wherever they wished, did not do so by dint of their money or their social position or because of whatever authority they arrogated to themselves of some fictitious nature; they did so by means of some sort of action outside of the social myths. Meaning, such tyranny with regard to social myths was a *new* tyranny. And it was a tyranny practiced against people already oppressed by social myths. It was, moreover, a tyranny practiced among themselves by people whose sincere purpose was nothing less than to destroy tyranny and to create liberty.

"Now transpose this situation to a much larger, much more influential group, already dealing with important questions and decisions of a fundamental character. Think of this group channeling its energies, like ours, toward the formation of a free society. And now tell me if, through a load of mixed tyrannies, you can envision any sort of society that seems to you to resemble a free society or any humanity worthy of the name. . . . "

"Yes, that's very curious. . . . "

"It is curious, isn't it? . . . And there are also secondary aspects to it that are very curious. . . . For instance, the tyranny of aid."

"Of what?"

95

"The tyranny of aid. There were those among us who, instead of commanding others, instead of imposing on others, on the contrary, aided them as much as possible. It seems to be the opposite thing, doesn't it? But look, it's the same thing. It's the same new tyranny. And, in the same way, goes against anarchist principles."

"That's a good one! In what way?"

"To give aid to someone is to judge that person to be a cripple; if that somebody is not a cripple, it's to make him into one or to assume he is one, which in the first instance is a form of tyranny and in the second, a form of disdain. In one it's to restrict the other's freedom; in the other, it's to depart, at least unconsciously, from the anarchist principle in judging the other worthless and undeserving or incapable of liberty.

"Let's return to our example. You see, of course, that the point is quite serious. Forget that we'd be working for a future society without anticipating that it would reward us, or, that we'd even be running the risk of its never coming to be. Forget all that. For what was worse would be to labor for a future of freedom and, instead of achieving it in practice, create tyranny, a new tyranny, a tyranny imposed by us, the oppressed, on others like us. Now this is what wouldn't happen. . . .

"I began to think about it. There must be something wrong here, some sort of mistake. Our goals were right; our doctrine seemed correct; was there something wrong with the ways we went about it? Surely that must be the case. But where the devil was the mistake? I began to think about this and almost went mad. One day, as always happens with such things, I suddenly hit on the solution. It was the great day of my theoretical anarchism, the day when I discovered, you might say, the technique of anarchism."

He looked at me a moment without seeing me, and then went on in the same tone.

"I thought as follows: . . . Here we have a new tyranny, a tyranny that doesn't stem from social myths. Then where does it come from? Does it stem from natural qualities? If so, goodbye to a free society! If a society where only men's natural qualities operate—such qualities as those men are born with, that belong to

96

Nature, and over which men have no control—if a society where only such qualities operate is a heap of tyrannies, who'd lift the smallest finger to help such a society come into being? Tyranny for tyranny, let's live with the one we've got, for at least we are used to it and therefore resent it less than we would a new tyranny that has that terrible character of all those tyrannical things that come directly from Nature—the impossibility of being able to rebel against it, just as there is no revolution possible against having to die, or against being born short when being born tall is preferred. Similarly, as I've already demonstrated for you, if for whatever reason anarchist society isn't practicable, then bourgeois society should be the one to go on existing, because it's more natural than any other.

"But does this tyranny that was born among us really stem from natural qualities? Then what are natural qualities? They are the level of intelligence, imagination, will, and so forth, that each of us is born with—this is clearly in the mental arena because there's no question now of natural physical qualities. The chap who dominates another, for reasons unrelated to social myths, does so demonstratively as a result of his superiority in one or another of the natural qualities. He dominates another by making use of such qualities. But now consider this: Is such use of natural qualities legitimate, that is to say, *natural?*

"So what is it to use natural qualities naturally? To serve the natural purpose of our personality. But would dominating someone else be a natural use of our personality? It might be. There's one instance in which it might be; that's when someone else is an enemy. For the anarchist, of course, the enemy is whoever represents social myths and their tyranny, and no one else, because all other men are men like himself and natural comrades. So now you can easily see that the tyranny we had been creating among ourselves is not of that sort; the tyranny we'd been creating was imposed on men like ourselves, natural comrades, and worse yet, doubly so, because they also shared in the communion of the same ideal. Conclusion: This tyranny of ours, if not derived from social myths, was similarly not derived from natural qualities; it derived from a mistaken application, from a perversion, of natural qualities. And where did that perversion come from?

"It had to come from either one of two things: either from man's being naturally evil, and therefore all his natural qualities would be *naturally perverted;* or from a perversion resulting from humanity's long sojourn in an ambience of social myths, all of them creations of tyranny and therefore already tending to convert instinctively from natural into tyrannical usage the most natural qualities. Now, of these two alternatives, which would be the true one? This was impossible to determine in a satisfactory fashion—that is, in a logical or scientific way. Reasoning could not enter into the question, as it was of a historic or scientific order, depending on a knowledge of the *facts.* Science does not help us because, as far back as we go in history, we always find man living under one or another system of social tyranny, and therefore always in a state that does not permit us to attest to what man is like when living in pure and natural circumstances. Having no way of distinguishing for certain between the two, we have to choose the more likely possibility; and the more likely is the second hypothesis. It is more natural to suppose that man's very long sojourn in an ambience of social myths created by tyranny causes each man to be born with natural qualities that are already perverted, that conduce spontaneously to tyranny—even if he doesn't want to be a tyrant—rather than suppose that natural qualities can be naturally perverted, which in a certain way is contradictory. That's why one who thinks about it must opt, as I do, with almost absolute certitude, for the second hypothesis.

"One thing is therefore evident: In the present social setup it's not possible for a group of men, however well intentioned they all may be, however dedicated they all are in fighting social myths and in working for liberty, to work together without spontaneously creating tyranny among themselves, without creating among them a new tyranny to supplement the social myths, without in practice destroying all that they wish for in theory, without involuntarily upsetting entirely the very purpose they wish to promote. What's to be done? It's very simple: It's for all of us to work for the same end, but separately."

"Separately?"

"Yes, haven't you followed my line of argument?"

"I followed it."

"And don't you find it logical, don't you find my conclusion inescapable?"

"I find it so, yes I do. . . . What I don't see is how this—"

"I'll make it clear. . . . I said we all work toward the same end, but separately. As all work toward the same anarchist goal, each contributes toward the destruction of social myths, which is where his effort is directed, and for the creation of the free society of the future; and working separately none of us can, in any way whatever, create a new tyranny, because no one can act upon another and therefore, in dominating him, can neither diminish his liberty nor, in assisting him, extinguish it.

"Working separately in this way and for the same anarchist goal, we have two advantages: that of a common effort, and that of not creating a new tyranny. We remain united, because we are morally bound and because we work in the same manner toward the same goal. We remain anarchists because each one works for the free society, but we cease to betray our cause, consciously or unconsciously; we also cease to be able to do so, because we place ourselves, by virtue of working for anarchism individually, outside of the deleterious influence of the social myths with their inherited reflexes upon the qualities that Nature endows.

"It's clear that such a strategy pertains to what I call the *period of preparation* for the social revolution. Once the bourgeois defenses lie in ruin and their whole society is reduced to accepting the doctrines of the anarchists, the only thing to accomplish then is the final blow, with the period of isolated action no longer possible to continue. For by then the free society will have virtually arrived; the state of things will have changed. The strategy I referred to only obtains to anarchist action in a bourgeois milieu, as it was with the group I belonged to.

"So I had finally found the true anarchist procedure. Together, we were not valuing what was important, and to top it all, we were tyrannizing one another and oppressing one another and what we stood for. Separately, we weren't perhaps getting very far,

99

but at least we weren't jeopardizing liberty or creating a new tyranny; what we were getting, little though it might be, was really a gain, without inconvenience or loss of any sort. And, furthermore, by working separately we were learning to have more confidence in ourselves, and by not leaning on one another, we were suddenly becoming more free to prepare ourselves for the future as much in our persons as others by example. . . .

"This discovery made me euphoric. I then went to explain it to my comrades. . . . That was one of the few times in my life when I was stupid. Just think, I was so full of my discovery that I supposed they'd go along with it!"

"It's clear that they didn't. . . . "

"They reprimanded me, my friend, they all reprimanded me! Some of them more, others less, but all of them protested: . . . That wasn't so! . . . This couldn't be so! . . . But nobody said what was so or what had to be so. I argued and argued, and in response to my arguments I got nothing but platitudes, garbage, the sort of thing bureaucrats say in committees when they have no answer at all to give. . . . Then I saw what jackasses and cowards I had to deal with! They were unmasked. That rabble was born to be slaves. They wanted to be anarchists at the expense of others. They wanted liberty as long as others would arrange it for them, as long as it was given to them, as a king hands out a title! Almost all of them were like that, those flunkies!"

"And you? You got angry?"

"Did I get angry! I was furious! I went into a frenzy! I came within a hair of using my fists on two or three of them. And I ended by taking my leave. I was isolated. You can't imagine how that flock of sheep nauseated me. I almost gave up believing in anarchism. I almost decided not to take all that stuff seriously. But after a few days I came to my senses. I regarded the anarchist ideal as being above such picayunish squabbles. So they didn't want to be anarchists. Well, I would be one. They just wanted to play at being libertarians. I was not someone to fool around with matters that important. They had no will power to fight except to lean on one another, creating among themselves a new simulacrum of the tyranny they wanted to combat? Well, let them do it, the cretins, if they were good for nothing else. I myself was not going to turn into a bourgeois for so little.

"It was established that under the new anarchism everyone should create liberty and combat social myths through his own efforts. So, through my own efforts I was going to create liberty and combat social myths. Did no one want to follow me along the right anarchist road? I myself would follow it. I would proceed alone with my resources, with my faith, unaccompanied even by the spiritual support of those who'd been my comrades, against all social myths. I'm not saying it was a fine or heroic gesture. If the road had to be followed by each individual separately, I had no need of anyone more in order to follow it. My idea would suffice. In these circumstances, based on such principles, I decided to combat social myths entirely by myself, alone."

For the moment, he interrupted his speech, which had become heated and fluid. A little later, when he picked it up again, his voice was more serene.

"It's a state of war, I thought, between me and the social myths. Very well, then. What is it I have against the social myths? I work by myself to avoid creating any sort of tyranny whatever. How can I alone collaborate in preparing for the social revolution, in preparing humanity for the free society? I must choose one of the two ways that exist, because clearly I can't take both. The ways are indirect action, that is, through propaganda, and direct action of whatever kind.

"At first I considered indirect action, which is to say, through propaganda. What sort of propaganda would I myself be able to carry on alone, aside from the sort one always does in talking with this and that person by chance and by seizing every occasion? The thing I wanted to know was if indirect action was a way I'd be able to go in order to channel my anarchist activity energetically, that is, a way of producing appreciable results. I then saw that this wouldn't do. I'm not a speaker and I'm no writer. I mean to say, I'm able to speak publicly and, when necessary, I can write a newspaper article, but what I wanted to find out was if my natural way of working indicated that, in specializing in indirect action, in which-ever of the two ways or in both, I might get *more positive* results for the anarchist cause than in concentration my efforts in another direction. For action is always more profitable than propaganda, except for those individuals whose talent marks them as being essentially propagandists—the great orators, able to electrify and pull the masses behind them, or the great writers capable of fascinating and convincing with their books. I don't think that I am very conceited or, if I am, at least I don't parade around the qualities I don't possess. And so, as I told you, I never set myself up as an orator or writer. That's why I abandoned the notion of indirect action as a way of fomenting anarchist activity. By eliminating the alternative, I was compelled to choose direct action—that is, an effort applied to the practice of living, to real life. It was not a matter of mind but of action. Very well. That's what it would be.

"Then I had to apply to real life the fundamental process of anarchist action that I had already made clear—to struggle against the social myths without creating a new tyranny but still creating, if possible, some semblance of future freedom. But how the devil is that done?

"Now what is it one fights in actuality? In actuality to fight means *war;* at least it's *some war.* How does one make war against social myths? Above all, how does one make war? How does one vanquish the enemy in any war whatever? In one of two ways: either by killing him, that is to say, by destroying him; or by imprisoning him, that is to say, by subjugating and reducing him to inactivity. I was not able to *destroy* the social myths; only the social revolution would be able to *destroy* social myths. Until then, social myths could be shaken, pushed around a bit, but *destroyed* only at the advent of a free society and the effective liquidation of bourgeois society. The most I could do in any such destructive sense was to destroy—in the physical sense of killing—one or another number of those classes representing bourgeois society. I studied the matter and saw that it was sheer stupidity. Suppose I killed one or two or a dozen representatives of social myths. . . . The result? Would the social myths be further weakened? Not at all. Social myths differ from political situations, which can depend on a small number of men or sometimes on one man alone. What's evil about social myths is that they exist in themselves, all together, and not in the individuals

102

representing them—except in that they represent them, of course. Moreover, any assault on the social order produces a reaction; not only do things remain the same but more often they grow worse. And, to top it all, suppose, as is natural, that after the assault I was captured—I was captured and liquidated in one way or another. And suppose I had done away with a dozen capitalists. How would all this end up finally? With my own liquidation; even if I weren't killed but simply imprisoned or deported, the anarchist cause would have lost an element of its struggle, and the dozen capitalists I'd have laid out wouldn't just be twelve elements that bourgeois society had lost, because the component elements of bourgeois society aren't combative elements but purely passive elements, because the 'fight' depends not on members of bourgeois society but on the totality of social myths to which that society gives its consent. So the social myths aren't people one can shoot. Do you understand that? It's not like I'm a soldier in the army killing a dozen soldiers of the enemy's army; it's like I'm one soldier killing a dozen civilians belonging to the nation of the enemy's army. It's killing stupidly, because it's not eliminating any combatants at all. ... I cannot therefore think of *destroying* either all or any part of the social myths. Consequently I would have to subjugate them, overcome by subjecting them, reducing them to inactivity."

He pointed the index finger of his right hand at me.

"That's just what I did!"

He let his hand fall and he continued.

"I tried to perceive which was the primary, the most important of the social myths. It would be the one that I would act on, more than on any other, to try to subjugate, to try to reduce it to inactivity. The most important, in our time at least, is money. How to subjugate money—or to put it more precisely, the power and tyranny of money? In liberating myself from its influence, from its power, in making myself superior to it, in reducing it to inactivity, by such means as concern me. Means that concern *me,* you understand, because it would be *I* who was fighting it: if I should have reduced it to inactivity with respect to everybody, that wouldn't mean to subjugate it but to *destroy it,* because that would have been to get rid of the myth of money entirely. Now I have already shown you that a social myth of whatever kind can only be 'destroyed' by a social revolution, pulled down with other myths in the downfall of bourgeois society.

"How was I to make myself superior to the power of money? The simplest procedure was to remove myself from its sphere of influence, that is, from civilization; go off to the country, eat roots, and drink water out of springs; go around naked and live like an animal. But that, even though doing it wouldn't be difficult, would not be fighting a social myth; it wouldn't even be fighting, it would be escaping. It's true that to avoid engaging in combat is not to be overcome by it. Yet it is being morally vanquished because it means not having fought. The procedure would be of that sort: It would involve combat and not the avoidance of combat. How to subjugate money by fighting it? How to divest oneself of its influence and tyranny without avoiding the need to meet it head on? There was only one way: *to acquire it,* acquire it in sufficient quantity to feel its influence no longer, and the more one acquired, the freer one would be from its influence. Only when I saw this clearly, with all the power of my convictions as an anarchist and with all my logic as a lucid being, did I embark on the real phase—namely, the mercantile and banking phase, my friend—of my anarchism."

He rested a moment from the newly rekindled impetuosity of his enthusiasm in telling of his discovery. Then, still with some warmth, he went on narrating his account.

"Do you recall now my telling you about those two logical difficulties that had arisen at the beginning of my career as a conscientious anarchist? And you recall that I told you that I then resolved them artificially by way of feeling instead of logically? ..."

"Yes, I do remember...."

"And you recall I told you that much later, when I finally found the true way of anarchism, I then resolved them—rationally, that is?"

"Yes."

"Now notice how I resolved them.... The difficulties were these: It is not *natural* to work for something, whatever it may be, without some *natural,* that is egotistical, compensation; and it is not *natural* to exert oneself toward any goal whatever without the compensation of knowing that *the goal is to be reached.* These were the two difficulties: Note now how I resolved them, thanks to my work as an anarchist, which my reasoning process led me to discover as the only authentic way. . . . The process ended with my enrichment, *consequently, an egoistic reward.* The process led to the attainment of liberty; for in growing superior to the power of money, and in liberating myself from it, I thereby *gained liberty.* Liberty, it's clear, only for myself; but as I already showed you, the liberty for all can only come with the destruction of social myths by the social revolution, and I cannot achieve that all by myself. The concrete point is this: I seek liberty, I get liberty; I get the liberty I can get because it's clear I cannot achieve the liberty I find unobtainable. . . . And please note: Even if one should set aside the reasoning process that resolves that this anarchist procedure is the only true one, the fact that it automatically resolves the logical difficulties that may be set against any other anarchist procedure proves certainly that this is the true one.

"I therefore have followed this particular path. I gave myself wholly to the undertaking of subjugating the money myth by getting rich. I succeeded. It took some time, for the struggle was great, but I succeeded. There's no point in going into what took place and what my merchant's and banker's life was like. It could be interesting, especially in certain aspects, but that isn't our subject here. I worked, I struggled, I earned more money; I earned a great deal of money, finally. I did not pay any attention to the means—I confess to you, my friend, that I did not pay attention to the means, but I employed them all—monopoly, financiers' sophisms, even unethical bids. And then some! I fought the social myths, immoral and antinatural par excellence, and is there any point in showing how?! I was working for liberty and I should have worried about the weapons used to fight tyranny?! The stupid anarchist who throws bombs and fires into crowds knows well he is going to kill and knows well that his doctrine excludes the pain of death. He fights immorality with crime, because he imagines that, in order to destroy immorality, crime may be thought salutary. He is as stupid as his act, because, as I've shown you, such a procedure is mistaken and counterproductive *as an anarchist procedure;* but as for the morality of the procedure, he is right. Now my procedure was correct, and I served myself legitimately, as an anarchist, by using all the available means to enrich myself. Today I have realized my dream, the circumscribed dream of a practical and lucid anarchist. I am free. I do what I wish, clearly, within the bounds of what's possible. My motto as an anarchist was liberty; well then, I have liberty, all the liberty it is possible to have in our imperfect society. I wanted to combat the social myths; I did so, and, what's more, I overcame them."

"Stop right there; stop there!" I said. "All that would be fine indeed, but there's one thing you don't see: The conditions of your procedure were, as you showed, not only to create liberty but also *not to create tyranny.* Now you created tyranny. As a monopolist, as a banker, as an unscrupulous financier—excuse me but you yourself said it—you have created tyranny. You created as much tyranny as any other representative of the social myths you say you were combatting."

"No, old chap, you're mistaken. I did not create tyranny. The tyranny that could have resulted from my combat action against the social myths did not issue from me; therefore I did not create it. *It stemmed from the social myths,* and I wasn't able, nor did I propose *to destroy* the social myths. For the hundredth time I repeat this to you: Only a social revolution can *destroy* the social myths; until then, perfect anarchist action, like mine, can only try to subjugate social myths, subjugate them only in relation to the anarchist who puts that procedure into practice, because that procedure does not permit greater subjugation of those myths. It's not a matter of not creating tyranny that's at stake; it's one of not creating new tyranny, tyranny that was not there before. The anarchists working together, influencing one another, as I told you, create *among themselves* a tyranny outside and apart from the social myths—that is, the new tyranny. That one I did not create. Nor could I have done so, besides, as the conditions of my procedure. No, my friend, I only created liberty. I liberated one man. I liberated myself. The procedure I followed, which is, as I showed you, the only true anarchist procedure, did not permit me to liberate more. What I could liberate, that I did."

"Fine. . . . I agree. . . . But notice that with such an argument people may almost be brought to believe that no representative of social myths imposes tyranny."

"And so he doesn't. Tyranny is found in the myths and not in the men who incarnate them; they are, so to speak, *the means* by which myths are used in order to tyrannize, in the same way that the knife is the means that serves the killer. And you certainly don't believe that abolishing knives abolishes the assassins. Look—you destroy *all* the capitalists in the world but *without destroying capitalism.* Tomorrow capitalism is in the hands of others; it will go on to perpetuate tyranny by such means. Destroy capitalism, not the capitalists; how many capitalists remain? . . . You see? . . . "

"Yes, you're right."

"My son, the maximum, the utter maximum you can accuse me of doing is that of adding a little— a very tiny bit—to the tyranny of social myths. The argument is absurd because, as I've since told you, the tyranny that I didn't have to create, and that I didn't create, is another thing. But you have another weak point: that is, by the same reasoning, you could accuse a general who undertakes to fight for his country of being the prejudicial cause of the death *in his own army* of a number of men he has to sacrifice in order to win. Whoever goes to war gives and takes. The main objective is victory, the rest . . . "

"That's all very well, . . . but now consider something else: The true anarchist wants liberty not only for himself but also for others. . . . It seems to me that he wants liberty for all of humanity. . . . "

"Undoubtedly. But I already told you that, according to the procedure I discovered as the only anarchist procedure, each one has to liberate himself. I liberated myself. I did my duty for myself and for liberty simultaneously. Why don't the others, my comrades, do the same thing? I didn't stop them. If I had stopped them, that would have been a crime. But I didn't for an instant hide from them the true anarchist procedure; from the moment I discovered the procedure I expressed it clearly to them all. The nature of the

107

procedure prevented my doing more. What more could I do? Force them to follow me? Even if I could do so, I wouldn't, because that would deprive them of liberty, and that ran counter to my anarchist principles. Help them? That too was impossible, for the same reason. I never have helped nor now do I help anyone, because that diminishes the liberty of another and likewise goes against my principles. You are really censuring me for not myself being more people who am one person only. Why censure me for accomplishing the duty of gaining liberty as far as I was able to accomplish it? Why not first censure them for not having accomplished their duty?"

"Well, man, all right. But if those chaps did not do what you did, naturally, it's because they are less intelligent than you, or have less will power, or . . . "

"Ah, my friend; now those are natural and not social inequalities. . . . Against such, anarchism can do nothing. An individual's level of intelligence or will power is between himself and Nature; social myths have nothing to do with it. There are natural qualities, as I've told you, which social myths may be assumed to have perverted through humanity's long sojourn among the social myths, but the perversion is not in the degree of quality, which is an absolute gift of Nature, but in the way the quality is applied. So a question of stupidity or lack of willpower shouldn't be viewed as an application of such qualities but only as a degree of the same. For that reason I tell you: Those natural inequalities are absolute, and no one has any power over them; nor is there any social change that would modify it, just as I could not myself become tall or you become short. . . .

"At least . . . at least, as far as those individuals are concerned, the inherited perversion of natural qualities hasn't progressed far enough to destroy the base of their temperament. . . . Yes, if an individual must be born a slave, he is naturally born a slave, incapable of the least effort to liberate himself. But in that case . . . in that case, what have they to do with a free society or with liberty? If a man is born to be a slave, then liberty, being contrary to his nature, will be for him a tyranny."

There was a brief pause. Suddenly I laughed aloud.

"You really are an anarchist," I said. "In any case, it makes me want to laugh, even after having heard you out, to compare what you are with what the other anarchists are. . . . "

"My friend, I've already told you, and I've already shown you, and now I repeat it: There's only one difference and it's this: They are anarchists only in theory. I am one in theory and in practice. They are anarchist mystics, and I am a scientific anarchist. They are anarchists who cower and cringe; I am an anarchist who fights and liberates. In a word, they are pseudoanarchists and I am the real thing."

And we rose from the table.

Lisbon, January 1922.

Always Astonished: A Journal

1. A Shrug of the Shoulders

We generally give our ideas of the unknown the coloration of our notions of the known. If we call death a sleep it's because it seems a sleep outwardly; if we call death a new life, it's because it seems something different from life. With small misunderstandings of reality we construct beliefs and hopes, and we love the crumbs we call cakes, like ragamuffins who jump around to be happy.

But all life is like that—at least the system of particular life generally called civilization is like it. Civilization consists of giving anything that does not belong to it a name and afterward dreaming of the result. And actually the false name and the true dream create a new reality. The object really becomes something else because we have made it other. We manufacture reality. Primary matter continues to be the same, but the form that art gives it effectively keeps it from continuing to be the same. A pinewood table is pine wood but also a table. We sit down at the table and it is not pine wood. Love is a sexual instinct, yet we don't love with the sexual instinct but by presupposing another feeling. And presupposition is, in fact, already another feeling.

I don't know by what subtle effect of light or vague noise or memory of perfume or music played by I don't know what external influence takes me smack into the street, and these divagations I slowly register on sitting down distractedly in the café. I don't know where I've been leading my thoughts or where I wanted to lead them. The day is warm and damp from the light fog, sad without being threatening, monotonous for no reason. It gives me some sort of feeling that I disown; some sort of argument is missing, about what I don't know; I have no volition in my nerves. In my subconscious I am sad. And I write these lines, really poorly recorded, not in order to say this, or to say anything else, but to give my wool-gathering some work to do. I am slowly filling with lackadaisical scrawls of a dull pencil, which I have no sentimentality about sharpening, the white wrapping paper used for sandwiches furnished me by the café because I needed nothing better and anything serves as long as it is white. And it satisfies me. I lean back. The afternoon falls dully and rainless, with its cast of gloom, uncertain light. . . . And I leave off writing because I leave off writing.

2. [The awakening of a city]

The awakening of a city, whether in fog or otherwise, is always for me more appealing than radiant dawn over country meadows. Dawn is much more renewing; there's much more hope when, instead of just gliding things, [there come] first the dark light, then humid light, then, later, brilliant gold, the grasses, the silhouette of the shrubbery, the palms with hands for leaves, the sun multiplying its possible effects on windows, walls, roofs . . . morning . . . with so many realities. A sunrise in the country makes me feel good; a sunrise in the city, good and bad, and that's why it makes me feel better than good. Yes, because the great hope it possesses brings me, like all hopes, that faraway and bitterly-longed-for taste of not being reality. Morning in the country exists; morning in the city promises. One makes for life; the other makes for thought. And I will always feel, like those great damned souls, that thinking is worth more than living.

September 10–11, 1931

3. [I'm riding in an electric trolley car]

I'm riding in an electric trolley car and slowly noting, as I habitually do, all the details of the people who pass before me. For me the details are things, voices, phrases. That girl's dress, as she passes before me, I reduce to the material it is made of, the work

112

that went into making it—although I see it as a dress and not as material—and the light embroidery that borders the part outlining the neck separates itself from me into the silk thread with which it was embroidered and the work necessary to embroider it. And immediately there unfolds before me, like a primer on political economy, the factories and the workers: the factory where the cloth was made, the factory where the silk thread was made of the darker thread they used to embroider the twisted little things into place close to the neck; and I see the sections of the factories, the machines, the workers, the dressmakers. My eyes turned inward penetrate the offices; they see the managers trying to look cool and collected; I follow the accounting of it all in the ledger book, but it's not only that: I see beyond it the domestic lives of the people whose social existences are lived in these factories and offices. ... The whole world is unrolled before my eyes only because I have before me, beneath that tawny neck, the other side of which I have no idea what face goes with it, an irregular regular dark green fringe on a light green dress.

All social life lies there before my eyes.

Besides this, I divine the loves, the soul secrets of all those who work so that this woman before me in the electric trolley might wear around her mortal neck the sinuous banality of a swatch of dark green silk on less-dark green material.

I'm stupefied. The trolley benches, made of a strong and interwoven small straw pattern, carry me to distant regions, multiplying themselves for me into industries, workers, workers' houses, lives, realities, everything.

I leave the trolley, exhausted and somnambulant. I have lived an entire life.

4. [These afternoons]

These afternoons I am filled, as a sea is at high tide, by a feeling worse than tedium but having no other name than tedium— a feeling of unlocatable desolation, of the shipwreck of my entire soul. I feel that I lost a complacent God, that the Substance of everything has died. And the perceptible universe is for me a corpse

I loved when it was alive, but it has all turned into nothing in the still warm light of the last colorful clouds.

August 22, 1931

5. [Suddenly]

Suddenly, as if magically destined to be operated on for an old blindness with great unexpected results, I raise my head from my anonymous life to understand clearly how I've existed. And I see that everything I've done, everything I've thought, everything I've been is a kind of delusion and madness. I'm amazed I never could see it. I find alien all that I was, which now at last I see is what I am not.

Like the sun breaking through clouds, I see my former life, noting with a metaphysical jolt that all my positive gestures, clearest ideas, most logical purposes are finally nothing more than born drunkenness, unadulterated madness, monumental ignorance. I wasn't even acting. I was enacted by them. I wasn't the act but the actor's gestures.

Everything I've ever done, thought, been is the sum total of submissiveness, owing either to the false creature I thought was mine because I impersonated it outwardly, or to the weight of circumstances that I supposed was as natural as the air I breathed. At this moment of seeing it, I am suddenly a solitary creature that recognizes itself banished from where it always thought itself a citizen. The being I thought myself most intimately to be, I was not.

Then some sarcastic terror of life overwhelms me, a depression surpassing the limits of my conscious individuality. I know I took the wrong path and went astray, that I never lived, that I existed solely because I filled time with consciousness and thought. And my sense of myself is that of one set free by an earthquake from the dim light of the prison cell he'd grown used to.

I am weighed down, really weighed down, as if condemned to recognize, by this quick sense of my real individuality, that I have always proceeded like a sleepwalker roving between what he feels and what he sees.

114

It's so difficult to describe what one feels when the feeling is that one really exists and the soul is a real thing that I have no idea what the human words are to define it. I don't know if I am in a fever, as I feel it—if I left off having the fever to be a sleepwalker all my life. Yes, I say it again, I'm like a traveler who suddenly finds himself in a strange town with no sense of how he got there, and I'm reminded of those instances of people who lost their memory and are not themselves for a long time. I was not myself for a very long time—from birth and consciousness—and now I remember leaning over the river from the middle of a bridge and knowing that I exist more firmly than I had until now. But the city is unknown to me, and the streets new, and the sickness without a cure. So I hope, leaning over the bridge, that the truth takes me and that I am remade as a fictive nullity with a lifelike intelligence.

It all happened in a moment; then passed. I see again the furniture around me, the design of the old wallpaper, the sunlight through the dusty windows. I saw the truth for an instant. For an instant of consciousness I was what the great men are in life. I recall their words and their deeds and don't know if they weren't also victoriously tried by the Demon of Reality. Not to know oneself is to live. To know oneself badly is to think. Knowing oneself suddenly, as in that lustral moment, is to have the sudden notion of an intimate monad, the soul's magical word. But the light suddenly singes it all, consuming everything. It leaves us naked, far away from ourselves.

It was just a moment, and I saw myself. Later now, I don't know what to say about what I was. And in the end I am sleepy, because—why I don't know; the sense of it is sleep.

February 21, 1930

6. Sentimental Education (?)

Whoever makes of dreaming a life, and of the hothouse culture of his sensations a religion and a politics, for such a one the first step—or what he charges his soul to take as its first step—is to feel trivial things extraordinarily and excessively.

115

... Whoever must live among people and be in active contact with them—and it's really possible to reduce to a minimum the intimacy one is obliged to have with them (the intimacy, and not simply contact, with people is what's damaging)—will have to freeze close association to its superficies so that all fraternal and social gestures made will slip by and not enter in or leave their imprint.

... To inject an immediate subtlety and complexity into the more simple and fateful sensations conduces, as I said, to augment immoderately the joy that feeling gives as well as to increase absurdly the suffering that will be felt. Hence the dreamer's second step should be to shun suffering. He should not avoid it like a stoic or an epicurean in the first instant—denesting himself—because he will thus harden himself to pleasure as well as to pain. On the contrary, he should search out the pain or pleasure and go on to educate himself to feel the pain falsely—that is, get to feel whatever pleasure there is from having to feel the pain.

... Another method, this one more subtle and more difficult, is to habituate oneself to embody the pain in a predetermined ideal figure. To create another "I" to be the one responsible for suffering in us, for suffering what we suffer. To create, then, some internal sadism, entirely masochistic, that enjoys the suffering as if it were someone else's.

... There is a third method to reduce pains into pleasures and make a soft bed out of doubts and worries. This is to give anxieties and sufferings, by an exacerbated application of one's attention, an intensity so great that it brings on, by its own excess, the pleasure of excess, just as violence suggests, to one habituated and educated in spirit to the vows and dedication of pleasure, the pleasure that hurts because it is so much pleasure, the joy that smells of blood because it has wounded.

7. [I've no idea of myself]

I'm one of those souls women say they love and never recognize when they meet, one of those souls that if they did recognize, even then they would not recognize. I suffer the delicacy of my feelings with disdainful attention. I have all the qualities for which the romantic poets are admired, even the fault of such qualities by which one really is a romantic poet. I find myself described (in part) in various novels as the protagonist of various plots, but the essential thing about my life, as about my soul, is never to be a protagonist.

I've no idea of myself, not even one that consists of a nonidea of myself. I am a nomadic wanderer through my consciousness.

8. Millimeters
(*Sensations of Minimal Things*)

Since the present is very ancient, because everything, when it existed, was the present, I harbor for things, because they belong to the present, the affections of an antiquarian preceded by the passions of a collector for whom my errors about things, having plausible and even truly-established and scientifically-based explanations, are dispelled.

... But it is only the minimal sensations, and of the minutest things, that I experience intensely. It will be through my love of the futile that this matters to me. It may be through my scruple for details. But in any case I believe—I don't know it; such things I never analyze—it's because the minimal, lacking any social or practical significance whatever, has, because of such a lack, an absolute independence of vulgar associations with reality. To me the minimal smacks of the unreal. The useless is beautiful because it is less real than the useful that extends and prolongs itself, while the marvelously futile, the gloriously infinitesimal, remains where it is—doesn't stop being what it is, lives free and independent. The useless and the futile open in our experience real intervals of aesthetic humility. In the heart of my dreams and amorous delights, how unprovoked I remain by the mere, insignificant presence of a needle stuck in a ribbon! How sad to be someone who misses the importance such a thing has!

... Blessed are the seconds and millimeters and the shadows of small things even more humble than they. The seconds ... the millimeters—what an impression of wonder and daring their existence side by side and so close to the metrical line rouses in me. Ah, the times I have suffered and enjoyed such things there. I take a crude pride in it.

I am an abundantly impressionable photographic plate. All details are engraved in me disproportionately in order to make up part of the whole. It's the all that concerns me. Evidently the external world for me is always sensation. I never forget what I feel.

1914

9. Zebra and Burro

I don't know how many will have contemplated, with the eye it deserves, a deserted street with people in it. This way of putting it already seems to mean something else, and indeed it does. A deserted street is not a street where nobody goes by but a street where passersby go along as if it were deserted. There's no difficulty in understanding this, provided one has seen it: A zebra is impossible for anyone who knows nothing more than a burro.

1932

10. [Living clotheshorses of uselessness]

Life for most men is a wearisome thing passed without taking account of it, a sorrowful thing made up of happy intervals, something like those moments when the deathwatch exchange anecdotes as they pass the still night with their obligation to the wake. I always found it futile to think of life as a vale of tears: It's a vale of tears, all right, but where one rarely weeps. Heine said that after great tragedies we always end by blowing our nose. As a Jew, and therefore [someone] universal, he clearly saw the universal nature of humanity.

Life would be unbearable if we made ourselves conscious of it. Happily we don't do so. We live with the same unconsciousness as the animals, in the same futile and useless way, and if we anticipate death, which might be assumed, though one can't be certain, we anticipate it by way of forgetting so much and with so many distractions and subterfuges that we can scarcely say we think about it at all.

So we live our lives, with little grounds for thinking we're superior to animals. Our difference from them consists in the purely external detail that we speak and write, that we have the abstract intelligence for both distracting ourselves by employing it concretely and by imagining impossible things. All those qualities, therefore, are accidents of our basic organism. Speaking and writing do nothing new for our primordial instinct to live without knowing how. Our abstract intelligence is of no use except in concocting systems or notions about half-systems rather than permitting us to be animals out under the sun. Our imagination of the impossible is not exclusive to us, because I've already seen cats staring at the moon, and I don't know whether they weren't yearning for it.

The whole world, all of life, is a vast system of the unconscious working through individual consciousness. Like passing an electrical current through two gases and making a liquid, so the double consciousness—that of our concrete being and that of our abstract being—makes a superior unconsciousness when life and the world are passed through it.

Happy the creature, therefore, that does not think, because it realizes by instinct and organic destiny what we all must come to see through subterfuge and inorganic social destiny. Happy the being that further resembles the brute, because it exists without effort by what we learn under pressure of work; because it knows the road home that we others don't find except through fictional shortcuts and regression; because rooted as a tree is, it is part of the landscape and therefore of beauty, and not like us, myths of the landscape, living clotheshorses of uselessness and forgetfulness.

11. Pigsties of the Soul

Aside from such common dreams ... are the shameful sluices of the pigsties of the soul that nobody will dare admit and that oppress insomniacs like filthy phantasms, viscosities, and greasy bubbles of the repressed sensibility, the ridiculous, the terrifying and unspeakable that the soul with some effort can still recognize in its crannies. . . .

The human soul is a madhouse of caricatures. If one could reveal itself in truth, without feeling a shame more profound than all the known and defined shames, it would be, as they say of truth, a well, but a sinister well full of vague echoes, peopled by ignoble lives, inert sliminess, slugs without being, snot of subjectivity.

12. [Unable to feel]

I play with my sensations like a princess totally bored with her great cats, swift and cruel. . . .

When we live constantly in the abstract—whether it be the abstraction of thinking or thought about sensation—before long and against our own feeling or will, we are turned into ghosts by those things of real life which, to be in harmony with our own selves, we would rather feel.

June 19, 1934

One of the great tragedies of my life—but one of those tragedies that transpires in shadow and subterfuge—is that of being unable to feel naturally anything at all.

13. [Ah, my unknown love]

Have you ever thought, you Other One, how invisible we are to one another? Have you ever considered how ignorant we are of each other? We see ourselves and don't see ourselves. We hear ourselves and scarcely listen to the voice within.

The words of others are errors of our hearing, failures of our understanding. How confidently we believe in our sense of the words of others. They smack of death to us, those pleasures others put into words. We read pleasure and life into words others let fall from their lips without their intending any deep meaning.

The voice of streams we interpret, . . . explaining, the voice of trees to whose rustling we give meaning—ah, my unknown love, how much of this is ourselves and ghosts made up entirely of ashes brushed off the gratings of our prison cell!

after 1913

14. Omar Khayyam

Omar had a personality; fortunately or not, I have none. What I am at one moment, the next moment separates me from; what I was one day, I forget on the next. Whoever, like Omar, is who he is, lives only in the world, which is external; whoever, like me, is not who he is, lives not only in the external world but in a successively diverse world internally. However much he wants his philosophy to be like Omar's he positively cannot make it be. Hence, without truly wanting them, I have in me, as if they were souls, the philosophies I criticize; Omar could reject them all, because to him they were external; I cannot reject them because they are me.

15. [Man is unable to see]

Man is unable to see his own face. This is what is more terrible: Nature gave him the gift of not being able to see it just as he is unable to stare at his own eyes.

Only in the waters of rivers and lakes could he stare at his face. And the position itself he had to take was symbolic. He had to bend over and lower himself in order to commit the indignity of looking at himself.

The creator of mirrors poisoned the human soul.

16. [In this metallic age]

In this metallic age of barbarians only a methodically excessive cult of our faculties of dreaming, analysis, and attraction can serve to safeguard our personality so as not to deface it, either by nullifying it or by being too much like the others'.

What is real in our sensations is precisely what they have in them of our not-ours. What's common in sensations is what forms reality. That's why our individuality in our sensations resides only in the enormous part of it. The happiness I would experience some day if I could see the scarlet sun! That sun would be mine and only mine!

Attachments like the china in a porcelain cup.
Reasons:
Our love affairs ebb quietly away, as she wishes, into barely two spatial dimensions.

17. [Modern things]

Modern things are:
1. the evolution of mirrors
2. wardrobes
We turn out to be clothed creatures, body and soul.

And, as the soul always corresponds to the body, the spiritual was established. We turn out to have an essentially clothed soul, whereby (men, bodies) we turn into the category of clothed animals.

It is not only the fact that our clothes become part of us. It's also the complication of such clothing and its curious quality of having almost no relation to the elements of the body's natural elegance or to any of its movements.

If you asked me to explain what the state of my soul is, assuming there's a sensible reason, I'd reply by pointing silently to a mirror, a hat rack, and a fountain pen.

18. Confiding, Confessing

The meanest of all needs—that of confiding, confessing. It's the soul's need to be external.

Confessing, yes, but confessing what you don't feel. Free your soul, yes, of the weight of its secrets by telling them, but still better than the secret you tell is never having told it. Lie to yourself before telling such a truth. To express yourself is always to go wrong. Be conscious: Let expressing, for you, be lying.

19. Maxims

Having definite and certain opinions, instincts, passions, and a known and fixed character—all this adds up to the horror of turning our soul into a fact, of materializing it, making it external. Living is a secret and fluid state of being ignorant of things and of oneself—and the only style of life appropriate and comforting to a wise person.

Knowing how to interpose oneself constantly between oneself and things is the highest level of wisdom and prudence.

Our personality must be unfathomable, even to ourselves; our duty then is always to keep dreaming and to include ourselves in our dreams so that it is impossible to hold opinions about ourselves.

And we must especially avoid the invasion by others of our personality. All extraneous interest is an odd indelicacy. What converts the common greeting *How are you?* into an unforgivable grossness is its generally being absolutely false and insincere.

To love is to be exhausted from living alone; it is, morever, a cowardice and a self-betrayal—it is supremely important that we keep away from love.

To offer good advice is to disrespect the God-given capacity of others to go wrong. It is scarcely comprehensible to ask advice of others—to know well is to act to the contrary; being in good self-accord, it is well to act in disaccord with Others.

20. Reflections

No age transmits its sensibility to the next; it simply transmits its intelligence of that sensibility. Through emotion we are ourselves; through intelligence we're someone else. Intelligence disperses us; that is why it's through what disperses us that we ourselves survive. Each age gives its successor only that which it was not.

A god, in the pagan sense—that is, in the real sense—is nothing more than the intelligence a being has of itself, since that intelligence it has of itself is the impersonal form of what is and therefore is the ideal form. In forming an intellectual conception of ourselves, we form a god of our very selves. Rarely indeed does one form such an intellectual conception of oneself, because intelligence is essentially objective. Rarely, even among the great geniuses, do those who exist for themselves possess full objectivity.

To live is to belong to another. To die is to belong to another. Living and dying are the same thing. But to live is to belong to another *from without,* and to die is to belong to another *from within.* The two things resemble one another, but life is on the other side of death. That is why life is life and death is death. The outside is always more truthful than the inside, inasmuch as it's the outside that's visible.

All true emotion is a lie to the intelligence, because emotion doesn't fit it. Accordingly, all true emotion is falsely expressed. Expressing oneself is saying what one doesn't feel.

The horses of the cavalry are what make up the cavalry. Without their mounts, the horsemen would be pedestrians. Place is what makes for locality. *Estar* is *ser.*

To feign is to know oneself.

21. [Always astonished]

I am always astonished when I finish anything. Astonished and depressed. My instinct for perfection should inhibit me until I get started. But I distract myself and do it. What I achieve is a product in me, not by applying my will but by giving in to it. I begin because I'm not motivated to think; I conclude because I haven't the nerve to leave off. The book is my act of cowardice.

The reason why I often interrupt my thinking with a passage about landscape, which in some way fits right into the scheme, real or imagined, of my impressions, is that such a landscape is a door through which I flee the knowledge of my creative impotence. In the middle of my conversations with myself, which form the words of the book, I suddenly feel the need to talk with someone else, and I address myself, as now, to the light that hovers on the rooftops of houses, which appear soaked in the light on their side; in the soft movement of the tall trees on the city slope that nearby seem threatening to crumble silently; on the posters superimposed upon the sloping houses with windows for letters where the dead sun gilds a humid gum.

Why do I write if I don't write better? But what would become of me if I didn't write what I manage to put down, however inferior to myself it may be? I'm a run-of-the-mill aspirant because I'm trying to get it done; like someone who dreads a dark room, I won't brave the silence. I'm like one of those who prizes the medal more than the struggle and enjoys the glory all wrapped in fur.

To write, for me, is to despise myself, but I can't stop writing. Writing is the drug I fight against and take, the bad habit I detest and from which I live. Some poisons are necessary and some most subtle, made of the soul's ingredients, herbs gathered in the recesses of the ruins of dreams, black poppies found at the foot of graves, long leaves from obscene trees that shake their branches at the whispering borders of the soul's infernal rivers.

22. Lucid Diary

My life: a tragedy broken to pieces under whistling and foot-stomping angels, and only the first act of it performed.

Friends: none. Just a few acquaintances who suppose they sympathize with me and maybe would be disturbed if a streetcar ran over me and the funeral was on a rainy day.

The natural reward for my estrangement from life was the inability I believed present in others to have any feeling for me. All around me was an aura of frost, a halo of ice that repelled others. Still I was unable to escape suffering in solitude. It is so difficult to achieve that distinction of spirit permitting one to be isolated in repose without anxiety.

I never credited the friendship shown me, because it would not be given with love if it were to be shown me, or because in any case it was impossible. Since I never had any illusions about those who called themselves my friends, I always managed to experience disillusionment with them, so subtle and complex is my destiny to suffer.

I never doubted but that they'd all betray me, and I was always amazed when they did. When what I anticipated did happen, I always found it unexpected.

As I never discovered in myself qualities attractive to anyone, I never could believe that anyone would be attracted to me. The view would be foolishly diffident if fact upon fact—those unexpected facts I expected—were not always seen confirmed.

Neither could I conceive that I was valued out of compassion because, being physically awkward and unacceptable, I lacked the degree of innate casualness with which to enter the orbit of others' compassion, or even to get the sympathy that attracts another when it is patently unmerited; and what in me merits pity is not available because there is never any pity for spiritual cripples. So that I fell into that center of gravity of strange disdain in which I was not inclined to anyone's sympathy.

All my life has consisted of wanting to adapt to this situation without feeling too much the cruelty and the abjection.

A certain intellectual courage is needed for a person to recognize boldly that he's no more than a human ragbag, an aborted survivor, a madman ever beyond the walls of the asylum; moreover, even great spiritual courage is needed, once this is recognized, in order to adapt perfectly to one's destiny [and be] accepted without revulsion, without resignation, without any gesture or trace of a gesture [indicating] the congenital curse Nature imposes on one. To wish not to suffer like this and wish it, moreover, because it is not humanly appropriate to accept the bad while seeing it as good and calling it good; and accepting it as bad, it is impossible not to suffer it.

Conceiving of myself from the outside was my misfortune—a calamity for my happiness. I saw myself as others saw me and grew to despise myself—not so much because I ought to recognize in myself such-and-such an order of qualities so as to deserve, through them, to be despised, but because I grew to see myself as others saw me and to feel my [own] scorn that they felt toward me. I suffered the humiliation of knowing myself. As this calvary promised no nobility or resurrection in the hereafter, I could suffer the indignity of it.

I understood that it was impossible for anyone to love me unless by default of all aesthetic sense—and then I would despise myself for this; and understood that even sympathy for me would not grow from a whim of extraneous indifference.

To see ourselves inside us clearly and to see in the ways others see us! To meet this truth face to face! And in the end the cry of Jesus Christ in Calvary when confronting his truth face to face: God, God, why hast thou forsaken me?

✖ Chronology

1888   Born Fernando António Nogueira Pessoa, June 13, in Lisbon.

1893   Father, Joaquim de Seabra Pessoa, a music critic, dies in Lisbon on July 13, at 43.

1895   Mother, Maria Madalena Pinheiro Nogueria Pessoa, marries by proxy João Miguel Rosa, Portuguese Consul to South Africa, and joins him in Durban with Fernando and uncle Cunha early the following year.

1896   He is enrolled in a convent school taught by Irish nuns in Durban. Stepsister, Henriqueta Madalena, is born.

1898   Stepsister, Madalena Henriqueta, is born.

1899   Enrolls in Durban High School.

1900   Stepbrother, Luís Miguel, is born.

1901   Accompanies his family on a visit to Portugal. Begins writing poems in English.

1902   Stepbrother, João, is born. Enrolls in a commercial (business) school in Durban.

1903   Takes the entrance exam to the University of the Cape.

1904   Returns to Durban High School and wins the Queen Victoria Prize with an essay on Macaulay (in English). The prize is a small library of books, including those of Milton, Shelley, Keats, Tennyson, Poe, Carlyle, and Jonson. Continues to write poems and prose in English. Stepsister, Maria Clara, is born.

1905   Returns alone from Durban to Lisbon, enrolls at the University, goes to live with his grandmother Dionísia and two aunts. Reads the English authors, especially Milton; also Baudelaire and Cesário Verde, and admits to continuing reading of "the Portuguese subpoets."

1906　Briefly rejoins his family, returns on a holiday to Lisbon. Stepsister, Maria Clara, dies in Lisbon.

1907　Goes back to live with his aunts in Lisbon. Leaves the University and starts a printing company, which fails.

1908　Embarks on his lifelong part-time work as a writer and translator of commercial letters.

1910　Founds the magazine *A Águia (The Eagle)* in Oporto.

1911　Undertakes to translate the Portuguese poets for a section in an anthology of world writers in English.

1912　Contributes literary and political articles to the Portuguese periodicals *A Águia* and *República.* His friend Mário de Sá-Carneiro, having left for Paris and the Sorbonne, publishes a volume of stories, *Princípio.*

1913　Writes an article in *A Águia* on the caricatures of the avant-garde Portuguese artist Almada Negreiros and gets to know him. Writes the closet drama *O Marinheiro (The Sailor)* and the erotic poem "Epithalamium" in English.

1914　Translates into English three hundred Portuguese proverbs for an editor in London.

1915　Writes an extended elegy in English, "Antinous," on the death of Hadrian's young lover. The first issue is printed of the influential magazine *Orpheu,* which he helps to found. Writes many of the poems of his heteronyms Caeiro, Campos, Reis, including "Saudação a Walt Whitman." Translates into Portuguese *Compendium of Theosophy,* by C. W. Leadbeater, the first of many books he will do for a series of theosophical and esoteric works.

1916　Sets up as an astrologer in Lisbon. Some weeks after writing Pessoa, Sá-Carneiro kills himself in a Paris hotel.

1917　Publishes privately in Lisbon two collections of his English poems, *Antinous* and *35 Sonnets,* in pamphlet form.

1918　Reviews of these pamphlets of poems appear in *The Glasgow Herald* and the *Times Literary Supplement* (London).

1919   Having announced the death of Alberto Caeiro on April 12, he writes a series of poems under that heteronym. Stepfather, João Miguel Rosa, dies.

1920   His poem "Meantime" appears in *The Atheneum* (London), and he finishes a group of English poems, *Inscriptions.*

1921   The long story "O Banqueiro Anarquista" ("The Anarchist Banker") is published in the first issue of the magazine *Contemporanêa.*

1925   His mother, D. Maria Madalena, dies.

1926   Applies for a patent on his invention, *Synthetic Yearly Calendar by Name and Any Other Classification, Consultable in Any Language.*

1927   The first serious critical opinion of his work (of "the master" Fernando Pessoa) appears in the magazine *Presença,* written by the young poet Jose Régio.

1929   An extended critical article on his work and personality appears in *Temas (Themes)* by the young novelist and critic João Gaspar Simões, who subsequently becomes Pessoa's earliest biographer *(Vida e Obra de Fernando Pessoa).*

1930   Starts a correspondence with Aleister Crowley in London.

1931   Translates Crowley's "Hymn to Pan" in *Presença* (Lisbon).

1933   Undergoes a severe psychological crisis. Prepares for the publication of Sá-Carneiro's book of poems, *Indicios de Oiro (Traces of Gold).*

1934   Wins second prize in a contest sponsored by the Secretariat of National Propaganda for his poem sequence *Mensagem (Message),* published the same year.

1935   Makes plans to publish his own first large collection of poems in Lisbon. Enters the hospital with hepatitis on November 28 and dies there two days later.

❊ Bibliographical Note

As there does not yet exist an authoritative edition of the complete works of Fernando Pessoa, the principal texts on which the translations are based have had to be drawn from various sources.

Fernando Pessoa. *Obras em Prosa*. Rio de Janeiro: Editora Nova Aguilar, 1982.

———. *Livro do Desassossego por Bernardo Soares*. Lisbon: Edições Ática, 1982.

———. *Textos de Crítica e de Intervencão*. Lisbon: Edicões Ática, 1980.

———. *Páginas de Estética e de Teoria e Crítica Literária*. Lisbon: Edições Ática, n.d.

———. *Páginas Íntimas e de Auto-Interpretação*. Lisbon: Edições Ática, n.d.

———. *Obra Poética*. Rio de Janeiro: Editora Nova Aguilar, 1983.

———. *O Banqueiro Anarquista*. Lisbon, Edições Antígona, 1981.

Other sources that were advantageous in translating and assessing material:

Fernando Pessoa. *Sixty Portuguese Poems* Introduced, selected, and translated by F. E. G. Quintanilha. Cardiff: University of Wales Press, 1973.

João Gaspar Simões. *Vida e Obra de Fernando Pessoa*. Lisbon: Livraria Bertrand, 1951 (rev. 1973).

George Rudolf Lind. *Estudos Sobre Fernando Pessoa*. Lisbon: Estudos Portugueses, Casa Moeda, 1981.

I am grateful for the assistance and good will shown to me by the poet's sister, D. Henriqueta Madalena Nogueira Rosa Dias, in all matters concerning this project as well as in everything preceding it.

E.H.

134

9 780872 862289